PENGUIN BOOKS

THREADING WORLDS: CONVERSATIONS ON MENTAL HEALTH
STORIES WE DON'T TELL

As an internationally recognised spiritual teacher, professional artist, social healer, life coach, and community leader, Hun Ming Kwang is relentless in his mission to illuminate individuals to their deepest truths, callings and authentic selves, helping them awaken and harness their power to actualize their lives at their highest creative potential. Today, he has helped over 10,000 individuals transform their lives and attain a higher level of awareness.

He also focuses on championing humanitarian campaigns and efforts to invoke and inspire awareness on social causes such as mental health and suicide prevention at a national level. He is the founder and co-artistic director of ThisConnect.today, where he designs and produces experiential art, interactive films and conscious conversations to make a difference to the public.

T0001598

OTHER BOOKS IN THIS SERIES

Threading Worlds:
Conversations on Mental Health
Stories We Don't Tell

Hun Ming Kwang

PENGUIN BOOKS

An imprint of Penguin Random House

PENGUIN BOOKS

USA | Canada | UK | Ireland | Australia
New Zealand | India | South Africa | China | Southeast Asia

Penguin Books is part of the Penguin Random House group of companies
whose addresses can be found at global.penguinrandomhouse.com

Published by Penguin Random House SEA Pvt. Ltd
9, Changi South Street 3, Level 08-01,
Singapore 486361

First published in Penguin Books by Penguin Random House SEA 2022
Copyright © Hun Ming Kwang 2022

ISBN 9789815058246

Typeset in Garamond by MAP Systems, Bengaluru, India

www.penguin.sg

Contents

Foreword

The latest Singapore Mental Health Study shows one in seven people has experienced some mental health challenges in their lifetime and more than 75 per cent of these did not seek any professional help[1]. *Threading Worlds: Conversations on Mental Health* Volumes seek to close this treatment gap.

The transcribed authentic voices of healthcare professionals and other community leaders and those with lived experiences will help us reach the self-realization of our own state of mental wellness. It will move us to co-create a safe space for the community to talk openly about the challenges and the solutions with courage and empathy.

One of the causes of the treatment gap is the stigmatization of the condition driving us from seeking treatment. I have been to ThisConnect's multimedia art exhibitions and one of the works, 'Connection without Sight', shows us how we can connect deeply through our primal senses and emotional centres without succumbing to the superficial judgement of sight.

---

[1] Subramaniam, M., E. Abdin, J. A. Vaingankar, S. Shafie, B. Y. Chua, R. Sambasivam, Y. J. Zhang, et al., 'Tracking the Mental Health of a Nation: Prevalence and Correlates of Mental Disorders in the Second Singapore Mental Health Study', Epidemiology and Psychiatric Sciences 29, 2020: e29. doi:10.1017/S2045796019000179

Active listening is essential for deep understanding with empathy without which the advice we give and receive are likely to be irrelevant and superfluous. Another work, 'I Feel You', will enable us to stand in the shoes of others and be there to hold that safe, sacred space for another human being.

Masks of Singapore, a six-month local community self-awareness mask-making project, depict the façade that most people portray to one another in our daily interactions. We wear these 'masks' to suppress our true mental state. The making of masks will help us discover our true self and give ourselves permission to express our truth more freely than ever.

This project is a cool way to create a healing place for us to courageously confront our own mental health challenges in a safe space. Wherever these books are found, a safe space to mine the comprehensive information leading one to seek treatment is created. I wish Ming Kwang and his team luck and may their endeavours be perfectly accomplished.

Dr William Wan, PhD, JP
General Secretary,
Singapore Kindness Movement

To You: A Message From The Author

Dear Reader,

If by a stroke of luck, a gesture of goodwill, something about this book resonated with you, it found its way to you, and landed in your hands—let it be a sign that there are certain answers in your life that you're searching for.

Before we begin, I would like to invite you to take a moment to picture this:

You're a student in your teens or early twenties. You're spending thousands of dollars on a formal education as you work your way up to a university degree, studying subjects only for the purpose of excelling in the exams, while juggling several other commitments such as an internship, a part-time job, an extra-curricular activity, to boost your credentials and show your potential employers that you have some degree of holistic development, real-world experience, and a life outside of your studies. Along the way, you might have countless nights of overwhelming stress, pressure, burnout, and negative downward spirals. You ask yourself endlessly: are you disappointing your family? Are you failing the expectations that others have of you? Are you on track to landing a stable job once you graduate? Do you have enough commitments on your plate to ensure you're not any less ambitious than your peers? Your teachers might have good intentions, but the most they tell you is 'Don't stress too much, just remain calm, be positive, be happy, and do your best'—as if those things never automatically occurred to you before. In a world full of adults who appear to have figured out all the answers to life, are you a failure if you can't be positive and calm without distracting yourself and numbing away your anger, sadness, and negativity?

This might also be the period where you struggle to make sense and find your place in your social world. How do people view you? Who are the friends who are going to stick by you as you enter adulthood and into the working world? Who are the people you need to be networking with so that you can position yourself favourably? If you don't manage to find a life partner now, will you still have the time and opportunities to do so once the rat race begins? Are you considered a failure if you never end up settling down with a partner and starting a family?

Or, perhaps you're a corporate executive or a full-time employee in your mid-twenties to thirties, working your daily nine-to-five job. When you first started out, you might have felt excited and driven to finally leave your mark on the world and fulfil your ambitions. But a couple of years later, your life has been entirely segmented into three parts: your day job, the couple of hours at night you have to rest before the next day, and the weekend, where you attempt to make up for all the rest, recreational activities, or social needs that you missed out during the week. Your job pays the bills, but it becomes a mechanical task for you to get through every day. It might not necessarily challenge you to grow as a person. It might not fulfil you, or it might not even be something in your interest in the first place—but you had no choice but to take it on anyway because the job market was bad, there was pressure on you to be doing something great with your life as a culmination of everything you've learnt after you graduated, and you spent nearly twenty years of your life studying and working relentlessly for a paper degree that only serves to tell your potential employers that you're knowledgeable and a specialist in that particular field of study. Surely you've got to work a job that justifies the amount of money, time, blood, sweat, and tears spent on your formal education at the expense of other pursuits that might be less lucrative, but more fulfilling! Otherwise, what did you give up your dreams for? And the unfortunate thing is, perhaps by the fifth year of your career, you're wondering if it is time to switch jobs or try your hands at something new. And for a while, it does bring a breath of fresh air into your life, but after a period of time, you find yourself back at the same spot again—stuck in an endless loop.

Perhaps you're a fifty-something veteran in your field, and you're looking for change, because you've gotten what you wanted out of your career and realized that there's something more you want out of your life. Perhaps you've realized that you neglected every other aspect of your life apart from your career, and you want to rectify that. Perhaps you're a seventy-something retiree, and you're wondering what else there is to life besides living it day by day as you wait for the day you die.

When you encounter such instances, when you question where your life is at, where it is going, what really matters to you, and what your purpose in life really is at the end of the day, I would like to assure you that it's a step you have taken towards looking inwards at yourself. And as much pain and struggle or joy and happiness as it may bring, **keep going**.

Sometimes, we give up our dreams and settle for less while telling ourselves that what we have is good enough. Sometimes, unfortunate circumstances happen to us and make us give up parts of ourselves. Sometimes, the life that we live does not belong to us, but to the expectations of us, to the intentions of others, and to the popular dreams that are trendy at the moment. We gather these second-hand dreams and ideas that belong to others and try to cobble together what our lives could be and what we desire. Be that as it may the answers don't lie there, but within us. However well and good our intentions are, in chasing after the lives of others, we reject and deny what is fundamentally at the root of ourselves: *ourselves*.

The term 'mental health' has rapidly gained traction over the last couple of years, especially in the wake of the pandemic, but there is still a large lack of understanding that mental health is a spectrum in which everyone has their own place depending on where they are in their journey. Some of us are battling mental health conditions and illnesses. Some of us are in the middle, where what we're going through is not necessarily deemed severe enough to be classified as an illness or disorder, but we feel the brunt of our symptoms nonetheless in our everyday lives, and it hinders us from thriving and performing at our optimum capabilities when we need to. Some of us are doing relatively well holistically in the different aspects of our lives, and we're looking at how to take it to the next level. Yet, as I say this, I want to emphasize that somebody who is thriving in their lives can absolutely still go through mental health struggles that are specific to their life's circumstances. Likewise, people who struggle chronically with mental illnesses or disorders can absolutely have days where they're feeling good. Essentially, everybody has mental health, and we relate to it in ways that are entirely unique to our circumstances, our psyche, and our history.

Where you fall on the spectrum is entirely unique to you, and that is why resolving your issues is not a matter of looking outwards at what people have done to resolve their issues and replicating that—although that can certainly give you more data and clarity on what works and what doesn't—but more importantly about looking inwards, understanding the true nature of the issue (since our external reality is really nothing more than a reflection of who we are inside), and examining the core of who *you* are, so that you can do what *you* need to do to triumph over *your* challenges and live *your* **best** life.

Presently, the world is going through a mental health epidemic. More than ever, people are experiencing increasingly severe bouts of depression, anxiety, and on the most severe end of the spectrum, suicidal thoughts, suicide attempts, and suicide cases. In fact, I want to highlight this particular incident that stands out to me. In 2021, a sixteen-year-old student from River Valley High School in Singapore was charged with the murder of a thirteen-year-old schoolmate. Our hearts sank when the news was publicly released. He was found to have been previously assessed at the Institute of Mental Health (IMH) in 2019 after attempting suicide. I believe that this incident highlights the state that children and younger folk are in these days in terms of their mental health and overall wellbeing. There is much more to be done and ground to be covered as this incident happened despite the increase of mental health and wellness programmes in schools and workplaces.

It is precisely because of this that we need to tackle the whole issue of mental health not by adopting a blanket one-size-fits-all solution, but by looking inwards, because suicide never happens in a moment. It never ever does. There are a million moments leading up to that point. Each moment we choose not to face and deal with questions that matter to or bother us, emotions that are 'unpleasant', or conflicts and baggage in our lives, we risk falling or spiralling further down the spectrum. Our issues never really go away until we deal with them and resolve them at the root level head on.

Our life begins the moment we're born—especially in the moments we can no longer consciously remember. The very first time you opened your mouth and cried out loud as a baby, what were your parents' reactions? What was *your* response to that?

The very first time you displayed any bout of anger or rebellion, what were the reactions of the people around you?

Did they talk down to you and reprimand you? Did your parents tell you that a good son or daughter would never have exhibited such behaviours? Were you present to the anger and the subtle shame and guilt that ran inside your programming? What did you learn about your emotions, social behaviours, and boundaries consequently from those incidents? The very first time you cried and wished you had your parents' approval and attention but was left waiting and wanting, what was *your* response to that? What did *you* tell yourself about love and relationships?

The very first time you opened up to a teacher or a family member about your dreams to be an artist, a singer, an astronaut, a designer, what was their response? What was *your* response as a reaction to that? What did *you* tell yourself about dreams and reality? What were *your* notions and beliefs around success?

Perhaps, this is about your identity. The very first time you realized that you fell somewhere on the LGBTQ spectrum, and you didn't exactly turn out exactly the way your parents or society expected you to be—'normal'—and you chose courage, came out to these people, but were rejected, or the first time you witnessed someone else in a similar boat get rejected and judged by others, what did it teach *you* about family? What did *you* tell yourself about *your* identity? What did *you* tell yourself about courage, and how did it shape your relationship with it?

One of the most common myths we have around pain is that time heals all wounds, but that couldn't be further from the truth. Time makes us forget that those wounds exist in the first place— it gives us the opportunity to evade or numb ourselves with drugs, alcohol, entertainment, or some other form of escapism from our pain, until we forget about them. And sometimes we go into a delusion thinking that these issues are no more. Silly us.

It doesn't matter what the topic is—the very first statements we tell ourselves about that topic, grows with us as we grow as people throughout the various stages of our lives, and they get reinforced over time as we encounter similar incidents repeatedly.

And oftentimes, while these statements may have served and saved us from pain once upon a time in the very first moment, they tend to do us more harm than good in the long run. For instance, if you've always been told that crying is bad and you were punished for it, you might have resorted to numbing away any nuance of sadness or grief the moment you feel it. Doing that might have saved you punishment from your parents while growing up, but as an adult, that numbing has its own repercussions. You might become so numb and disconnected from yourself that you can't tell what matters to you anymore, and you're always looking outwards for answers. Each time you suppress an emotion just adds another drop into the pressure cooker of emotions inside you that's bubbling and waiting to explode when you least expect it, and when you're least prepared to deal with it.

Emotions have always been a tricky topic that we've not yet managed to successfully incorporate well into our upbringing at home and in the education system. Our understanding of emotions is largely limited to happiness, anger, and sadness, but what about everything else in between? What about the subtle emotions like guilt, jealousy, shame, disgust, contempt, or envy? Not to point fingers at anyone in particular, as most parents and educators are only teaching what they've been taught and what they know, and we simply do not know any better, but some of the most unhelpful advice given to kids in school regarding emotions is to just 'not be sad because it doesn't help' and 'be positive and things will work out'. What we've gotten out of that advice are generations of people who are completely out of touch with their emotions, particularly those that are deemed as 'difficult and unpleasant', and are going through the motions of their lives without ever fully participating, engaging, and involving *themselves* in how it unfolds. This only serves to worsen the mental health struggles we face and potentially turn them into long-term mental health disorders.

The unconventional wisdom is to be able to receive the pain such that the pain completes its course. And when the pain no longer has a reason to make you suffer, then perhaps it's time for you to heal. And if you are not busy dying, maybe you will expend some energy into what it takes to live. And if you live, the next question is, how alive do you want to be?

It is crucial to understand that having the ability to manage our emotions is tantamount to managing ourselves as people who are functional and able to contribute value meaningfully to society. It is integral to be able to deal with crisis situations, to being able to lead and work with a team of people from all walks of life with various personalities. It is necessary to be able to connect with another person on a deeper level and hear the things that are left unsaid. It is absolutely paramount to maintaining a healthy overall wellbeing, because a heavy suppression of our emotions eventually leads to the damage on our physical body that manifests as various forms of diseases and illnesses.

The repercussions and consequences of not being able to deal with crisis, of not being able to deal with people both in our personal and professional lives, of having our emotional baggage manifest itself as physical diseases such as cancers, diabetes, or even autoimmune diseases can leave a deep negative impact that takes us years to recover from. Some people never really quite recover. Some resign to the fact that their life is filled with woes so much so that they have accepted that this is where and how their lives end, and these are the people who unfortunately never come to the awareness that there is a way out.

I want to say this: **There is always a way out, no matter how bad circumstances present themselves to you**.

Fortunately, if you're finding *yourself* and looking for *your* place in this world, there is a way—your mental and emotional health is a starting point from which you can begin looking into your psyche, your past, your present, how your future will play out, and what you can do NOW to shape them—just as you shape your life, your paths, and your destinies.

Threading Worlds: Conversations on Mental Health is a literary compilation of conversations my team and I had with seventy-five other contributors in Singapore from March 2021 to May 2021 around the topic of mental health and emotional wellness. These seventy-five contributors come from all walks of life—doctors, nurses, caregivers, counsellors, psychiatrists, therapists, policymakers, social workers, politicians, business leaders, coaches, and youths—and we had facilitated conversations with them on their perspectives on the mental health scene, their own personal journeys, as well as what needs to be done at an individual, community, and national level so that we can move forward and evolve as a collective. Each conversation was transcribed word-for-word with minimized filters deliberately to retain the essence of each conversation such that readers are able to immerse themselves in the conversation and experience it as though they were present in the very moment when the conversation first took place.

This book is intended to serve as a mental and emotional health literacy resource worldwide, and especially in countries like Japan, Korea, and Thailand, where suicide rates are the highest, and the third-world countries where looking inwards and the whole idea of mental health is a luxury in relation to the survivalist fights they have to battle each day instead. Through the perspectives from different walks of life, stories of vulnerability and journeys of recovering and rediscovering oneself, instead of telling people what mental health is and what it is not, we aim to create an immersive experience that allows you to connect to yourself and derive the personal wisdoms and lessons embedded within these stories with your inner-knowing that you can apply to your life. It is best experienced in a distraction-free state when you are able to be *fully and wholly present to yourself* as you experience the book.

As much as you are able to at this moment in your life, I would like to invite you to begin approaching this not exclusively as a mental-health-specific topic, but as a journey of illumination that you embark on to seek the important answers to the questions you have about yourself, your life, and the world around you, so that you can find your footing and live a life that truly matters to you at the end of the day. Many of us, at some point in our lives, ask the bigger questions with heavier weights: Who am I? Where did I come from? What am I meant to do? What is my purpose? What is my truest self? What is the meaning of life itself? And what about my life? How do I live a worthwhile life?

That is right. This has always been about your life, not just your mental health. When we run so hard trying to find our way out of the overwhelming barrage of circumstances our lives are presented with, we might find ourselves reaching our breaking point and collapsing physically, mentally, emotionally, even spiritually. At times when we are defeated, there is no way upwards but to muster every drop of willpower in us to crawl our way to the door and roll ourselves out.

We live in a world where our actions create a ripple effect down the road. Consequently, there are the forces of cause and effect in play. What matters is not what happens in the past or the future, but what you choose to do right now that consequently affects the trajectory of your life. Every passing moment is a second chance to turn it all around. As the saying goes: 'It is easier to build strong children than to repair broken men.' For us to nurture a generation free from the weight of the pain that we and our ancestors bear, we must first heal ourselves to break out of the chains that bind us. To find ourselves, we must first have the courage to give up what we believe is the truth about ourselves and walk the path of self-discovery. Only then do we know what it takes to make a difference to ourselves, and can we have the power to teach others what it means to be a human being in their own right, and be that beacon of light to those finding their way out of the dark.

Ultimately, my goal is to see a society where people thrive, not just survive, and are empowered to be bold, be free, and be ourselves. To have a conscious connection, not just with another person, but with ourselves. To embark on a journey to seek the answers we're searching for. To dare to dream, and dare to make those dreams happen. To gather our courage and take leaps of faith, even if we don't know where and how we'll land. To confront our deepest fears. To stand on the roof and declare our deepest truths to the world. To strike a pose and shout out to the universe, 'This is Me!' To challenge our adversities. To fail in our quest to live a good and fulfilling life, because it is through those failures that we learn what it means to stand for something that matters to us, time and time again, against all odds. To feel deeply, love deeply, and know that there is absolutely no shame in expressing ourselves authentically, no matter what people think.

One life saved can save many other lives. When we embark on the journey of living a life that truly matters to us, we also empower ourselves to step onto a path that enables us to touch another person's life with our highest being. A path along which we create a future that we're excited to step into, a path where we *leave our mark* on the world—so that when the time comes for us to go, we will go not with regrets, but with the knowledge that we have given every drop of our tears, sweat, and blood to living a life true to ourselves.

All of us are a walking morass of questions, on the journey of seeking the answers to living fully alive, and enjoying the ride along the way. Again, to reiterate what I said in the beginning—if by the stroke of luck, a gesture of goodwill, something about this book resonated with you, found its way to you, and landed in your hands—let it be a sign that there are certain answers in your life that you're searching for, and may this book contain some of the lessons and wisdom that can empower you on this journey. When you are done, pass it to another person to pay it forward.

Because you never know who may need just that ounce of light to get themselves back on track, since we have adapted to become experts in masking our emotions (I say this sarcastically . . . but this is a very real issue today).

I share this message from a space of love and courage, as somebody who has taken a stand for the transformation of ourselves, transcendence of our limitations, and actualization of our innate potential. And when the time comes, I look forward to meeting you, the reader of this book, someday—the parts of you that can be a beacon of light to the higher consciousness of this world. May our stories, journeys, and collective wisdoms and transformations inspire even more people to begin looking into themselves so that they can begin their own journey of transformation, so that they live their marks on this world, so that when the time comes for us to go, we will go not with regrets, but with the spirit of the life that we've lived well with dignity.

Hun Ming Kwang
Founder, Creative Director, Author of ThisConnect.today

CHAPTER 1

In Memory of a Friend Lost to Suicide

By Lynette Seow, Chief Operations Officer, Safe Space

Lynette lost a close JC friend to suicide seven years ago. She shared her story of how difficult it was to deal with the grief of losing her friend, and all the conflicting emotions that came with it. Lynette also shares her thoughts on some of the myths about suicide based on her own experience. As a bereaved individual, she talks about the importance of being open to the difficult emotions we may be dealing with, and to asking for help when we need it.

I WAS NOT PLANNING ON A FULL-TIME CAREER IN MENTAL HEALTH

MK

Lynette, what made you decide on this career path?

Lynette

I officially joined Safe Space in January 2021 but I helped out as a volunteer since July 2020. I've always been interested in psychology, how the mind works, how people function, since forever. I guess the incident for me that prompted me wanting to go into it, and not just thinking about it as a fun academic topic, was actually getting a call one night in September 2015.

My friend was like 'Hey, are you sitting down?' I was like 'No, I'm out, what's up?' And he's like, 'Oh, sorry to tell you but somebody has passed away'.

'Your friend has passed away.'

It was our common friend from secondary school. The first instinct was to ask questions, right? *Why? What? What happened? How do you know?* That kind of stuff.

The next few days and weeks were insane. Alina[2] had committed suicide and that made it a very tangible topic for me. In a way, it wasn't surprising. But at the same time, I wondered if there was any way this outcome could have been avoided. So that prompted a journey of starting to speak about mental health more openly, more personally, recounting this story, recounting its effect. Every time I talk about this since September or October 2015, everybody I've spoken to has said that they know somebody close to them who either has also committed suicide or is struggling and they're worried for them. *Everybody.* It's crazy. So that was where I was at for the next two, three years after that.

---

[2] Name has been changed to protect identity

Because of a change in job role and saving on travelling time while working from home during COVID, I had more time to look at the mental health industry globally last year. I started thinking about it more—very millennial. *What do you want to do with your life?* And I just identified mental health as a cause that I would be proud of, that I would be satisfied with my life if I spent however many years I have making a difference in this area. So I started doing some research—what's going on in the industry, *blah blah blah*. I had heard of Safe Space a couple of years ago very early on. I think there was barely even a Minimum Viable Product then.

I was like 'Hey, why not? Let me just ping the founder'. I contacted her on LinkedIn and said 'Hey, I have some free time right now, this is my CV, can I help out in any way? No intentions, I'm not looking for anything. I just want to get plugged into the space because I'm interested in it and want to know how I can contribute'. So I started off helping out with building the current tech product and then it worked out so well. I LOVED what I was doing every day. It wasn't supposed to even be every day. It wasn't supposed to even be any kind of commitment! But I felt like, *hey I can't imagine not making this my life's work!* So things kind of escalated, worked out so well, and I jumped in officially in January 2021.

[laughter]

Lynette

So kudos to Anto, the founder, who ensured that I got really integrated with every part of the company and decision-making from the start.

It was a very easy choice for me. *Do you want to continue on with your corporate job* (I was in tech consulting) *or do you want to take a chance on something that you enjoy doing, that makes a difference, that you can really live out passionately and purposefully every day?* And I guess you guys can empathize with that or understand that.

THE AFTERMATH OF SUICIDE

Si Qi

I wanted to know a little more on your story about your friend; and I'm sorry for your loss. What was it like to find out about the news and the aftermath of that? What kind of reflections did it spark in you about mental health and suicide?

Lynette

So many!

It's a long story. It was a whole process. I think honestly . . . It might have taken me about five years to come to terms with it in some sense.

The immediate aftermath was to inform everyone. *Who knows? Who do we inform? Who was close enough? Is it too personal or shocking? What do the parents want? What does the family want?* And back in school, the family wasn't huge fans of us. They're very private. There was a divide between us—her closest friends, and her family. We felt like . . . how do we respect them while honestly still being a bit angry at them because although it's harsh to say, but at that time, we did attribute some kind of blame, almost, to them. So there was that.

We were also trying to figure it out ourselves as a group. We were very close in secondary school and junior college. Drifted apart in university. This happened one to two years after we had graduated and had just started our jobs. *Who do we call? Who do we inform?* We didn't really know what to do. So what we did was just to gather the next day, recount the different angles of the story of how whoever found out, found out.

Basically, Alina had sent a box with some memorabilia from secondary school to one of our friends. She then flew to meet another friend in Hong Kong. It happened in Hong Kong. She met one of those friends working in Hong Kong for a last dinner almost, and then took some pills in her hotel. The way the whole plan was executed was very elaborate.

There were bits of other hints almost that had been released along the way. All of us had kind of almost gotten different pieces of a puzzle and we were just trying to piece it together after that. And we kind of drifted apart in university, so this was the first time in a long while that we all came together in a shitty situation. So yeah. It was a lot of just trying to make sense of what happened.

Then the next phase was . . . So we weren't invited to the funeral, that was a completely closed-door event. We had our own memorial for her separately. Went to Sentosa, got a room, went to the beach, brought things that were memories for us, made a time capsule, all that kind of stuff. And grieved. Just basically grieved. Um . . .

[silence]

Lynette

And I think during that point, three weeks to a month later, I recognized that everybody grieves differently and processes the same situation differently. Some of them would be like, *Could I have done more? Should I have gone down to a place this particular night when I knew she was not in a good state? It wasn't the same night but maybe I should have been down there? Or should I have kept in contact more? Should I have done something more?*

My take on it was always . . . Actually, I don't know whether it has changed now. My perspective then was I guess, knowing her, I always thought it was inevitable. It was not . . .

[pondering]

Lynette

It wasn't realistically fathomable in my head that it would actually happen, but when she did decide to do it, it's almost like you cannot imagine it any other way. Just that kind of person.

So I think . . . I didn't feel any guilt or anything. It was just pure grief. So that was that. And then there was a formal memorial that the family invited us to.

[silence]

Lynette

It was held in a traditional church. While a lot of us came from church backgrounds, we also knew her struggles with the church; so we were not the biggest fans of her family or her church friends and that whole ecosystem. There was a service. Her dad went on stage to give a eulogy. I remember being very angry (laughter) when I heard it. Because his eulogy read like a CV.

[silence]

Lynette

And I was just thinking, *My God! Do you even know your kid?* It was just like, she went to this school, she went to this school, she got into law school and decided not to take it up and ended up doing film instead. It just read like a CV. So on one hand there was anger, but on the other hand it's just . . . I mean it's sympathy, I think. Balls. That guy lost his daughter, right? So you can't be angry at him for long. He looked absolutely shattered.

MK

Yeah.

Lynette

Then I gave a eulogy on behalf of the secondary school friends.

So her mum had contacted the friend that she met in Hong Kong for the last . . . the last supper. Her mum asked if any one of her friends could do a eulogy. That friend didn't want to do the eulogy, and so she asked me and I agreed. It was like, I didn't know what else to do, right? I thought it was something I could do. I mean, that helped me in the grieving process also because I think if I just sat around . . . My objective for that was just to show her friends, her family, a glimpse of the person I had the privilege of knowing. That we all did. We had our best times in school together doing nonsense things. I had to really dig deep and think of all those stories, those incidents that just came to mind. They did not necessarily impact me in any tangible way, not like she said something and then my life course changed. But it's just things we took for granted like seeing each other in school every day.

Like a friend came up with a stupid game of blowing plastic bags around the corridor and seeing who could do it fastest. Something ridiculous that you'd probably expect from five-year-olds, not fifteen-year-olds. Haha!

[laughter]

Lynette

But Alina was the only one who was game enough to play and not make that friend feel stupid for coming up with such a random idea.

I think the incident for me was when I was angry about something and I just went to fume by myself at the football field. I just sat there, staring into space, and when I was done fuming and got ready to go back to class or whatever, I turned around and realized that Alina was sitting behind me the whole time. We're both very similar in terms of the fact that we didn't like to talk, especially about feelings. Very Asian, huh? But she was just waiting for me to be done with whatever I needed to process as a sign of solidarity. Yeah, so just stories like that.

I just enjoyed telling stories like that for the whole ten minutes or however long it was. And then three of us performed a song item where we mashed her favourite songs. She's into music very much. So we chose songs that both helped us express the grief and solidarity we were feeling, and also a touch of just reminiscing and celebrating the good times. We performed, did a second item, and then there was one more eulogy by her church friends. That was the end of the memorial.

I remember at the end, I turned to one of our secondary school friends and asked, 'So what's next?' We had basically thrown whatever we could have into grieving and processing. But we're not done. There is still a gap. There's still this hole. There's still this, *what next?* I guess the years after, we all went about it in different ways.

I remember the immediate few months after that; for sure there was a lot of drinking, haha! A lot of smoking, a lot of all the vices that we just needed to forget or avoid. Some processed by speaking more, recounting more stories. Personally, I had trouble saying her name. This was something that was very hard for me for I don't know . . . I don't know how long. Yeah . . . Just the name.

[silence]

Lynette

Eventually as time went by, quite a few years now, it was nice that there were people in the group who could bring up incidents with her. Or like *oh, this new place that we're checking out, Alina would have loved it.* She still is always part of the group.

[silence]

REFLECTIONS ON MENTAL HEALTH AND SUICIDE AS A BEREAVED FRIEND

Si Qi

What were your reflections on mental health from this incident?

Lynette

So I told you that when I was first processing it, I thought that this was inevitable. I think because to me, it was knowing how she was, knowing that her personality was a pretty depressive one. It was a logical conclusion or a way to go. If it didn't happen, it was luck, almost.

Many things have changed since this incident, and I constantly have new thoughts and reflections about what happened. So a few things.

Being able to ask for help, give help, receive help, is something that needs a lot more attention. That's why you're doing this to reduce stigma and all that, right? We don't have to wait until it's really late to ask for help. I guess just starting early and just being more open. That's something I've been learning since working with Safe Space. There's so much power in being open both for the individual who is being open as well as for the people who hear the stories. And that's part of the reason why I told Anto that I wanted to do this project with you guys. I mean the fact that everybody I spoke to since 2015, all had a personal story of at least a direct friend or family member who was struggling with mental health says a lot about how common this actually is.

It's like a generational pandemic. It's just part of the human condition. Everybody has health. Sometimes it's good. Sometimes you get a cold and you're not well. That happens as well, mentally. We expect people to be functioning almost the same every day, but it doesn't work that way. You're just not in the same mental state each day.

Not being ashamed to talk about your mental health is one thing. It's also about knowing how to respond. Like I said, when I got the call, it was not a surprise. Which means this was something that was coming at least ten years ago, or something that had its seeds planted nearly ten years ago. It definitely didn't have to be that outcome. My group of friends were very good with being supportive, like 'If you need anything just let us know, we won't judge you' or whatever, right? But it's still hard for people to talk about it. So how can we enable the average person to be able to prompt questions to help people have those conversations?

The first line of defence almost isn't a therapist. It's your colleagues, your friends, your family members, people you meet every day. And how can we recognize it? I think a tendency is that even if we suspect something, we don't want to call it out. Very Asian, very Singaporean. So how do we reduce the stigma on both sides to not be shy to call it out and just ask what's up? And on the receiving side, how do you decide to say 'Hey I'm not doing so well today?'

THE PAIN NEVER REALLY GOES AWAY

Si Qi

You mentioned that though the outcome for your friend was difficult to prevent, it didn't have to be that way. Could you share your thoughts on that?

[silence]

Lynette

It's about finding an angle to think about things, right?

[silence]

Lynette

Yeah, it's about finding a . . . Not say what can you contribute, that's very utilitarian, but . . .

[silence]

Lynette

I think there is always an angle to be discovered. To find meaning in life. And it's not easy.

There are people who are not suicidal and do not know what their meaning or purpose in life is. There are extreme cases as well—let's leave euthanasia out of the discussion. But for a regular person, I think something like making a difference to other people's lives is meaningful to a lot of people. We don't have to do something big to make a difference in people's lives. It's not a numbers game. It's whether you can make a difference to one person's life. And we had this conversation previously, right?

MK

Yeah.

Lynette

You said you're not looking for numbers either. If it saves one life, that's it, that's more than enough. And very often we mean a lot more to the people around us than we know.

Another learning from this was . . . It's almost like when you're in a group of people who are drunk, the fastest way to sober up is if you have to look after somebody. If you have been left behind by somebody who has committed suicide, you would never want to do it yourself. Okay, maybe it's just for me. Everybody thinks differently, right? Because you see the . . .

MK

The consequences in real time. And you know the pain.

Lynette

Yeah, you see the pain of everybody around you. You never . . .

MK

As a bereaved . . .

Lynette

Yeah. The consequences are . . .

MK

You see the aftermath, the impact from different dynamics, from a personal relationship, to groups, to community, to family.

Lynette

Yeah. There was an actual impact to whoever's left behind. You just see how shattered people around are, but you could never imagine inflicting that pain on somebody else.

MK

They say time heals all wounds, but it's not true, isn't it?

Lynette

Seven years on, as a group of friends, we still send her mum flowers every year during her birthday. Because you know, everybody's still hurting. That's the way that we know how to do something about it. It's our way of saying, 'Hey, her life is not forgotten, we're celebrating her birthday and we're still thinking of her'. It wasn't a memorial and done, I'm outta here. Because that pain, people will carry with them the rest of their lives. So there's gotta be a better option.

LOVE, EXPLICITLY.

MK

If you could have a message for people out there, what would that be?

[silence]

Lynette

I would say, be explicit in loving and caring for the people around you.

I guess with depression you feel alone. The most common feedback that we get from our clients here is that 'the therapist is able to provide me with a listening ear'. These are fairly regular people you see everywhere. They should have listening ears among their family and friends. Why should they need somebody else to do that for them? But because culturally and all that, we do tend to withhold love, or we're very shy about being explicit about it. Therefore, that builds up this sense of isolation, when that's not really the case. Being explicit creates an environment where the individual who is suffering feels that it's okay to reach out, that it's fine to say 'I'm in not my best state', that it's okay to be whoever they are in terms of whatever they're struggling with.

Can you imagine? This is my closest suicide case but it's not the only one I've seen among acquaintances.

[silence]

Lynette

If let's say 100–200 people turn up for your memorial, don't you think one of them would listen? That's ridiculous, right? That there was no one whom you could have turned to for whatever kind of support. Maybe accompany you to a psychiatrist should you need medical intervention. Point you in the right direction. Or just ask you, check in with you, 'How's it going today?'

I think a lot of people would rather . . . be okay to put in the effort and be around rather than doing the best they can when they attend a memorial. So, my message would be to be explicit in expressing your love to the people you care about.

Because you might assume that those around us know but they still need to experience it.

[silence]

HOW ARE YOU FEELING?

MK

How are you feeling?

[silence]

Lynette

My whole journey in the last six-seven years has been about making sense of that death. And making the best with whatever can possibly come out of it. This is why I do what I do. But somehow, getting personal and actually talking in so much detail about the story publicly is probably unthinkable. Heck, even last year. Everybody working in mental health has a story of why they're doing it. I remember when that was asked of me, I used to start off by saying that 'I did a lot of research in this area in the industry, I think this is a great business opportunity'. I was going from the angle that it made sense as a market opportunity. It took me a few months before I could start talking about the real reason.

I remember the very first time I said it out loud in some mangled way. I couldn't sleep at night. I was so uncomfortable. I've talked a lot today about being open and all that, but it's not easy. It's not easy for a lot of people to do, but it's almost like a habit, a muscle. To learn how to continuously be open and think with the motivation that you don't know who you can help by being open. By being closed, there's almost nobody you can help.

So how am I feeling, right now? Batshit scared, man. I was before this as well. But also at peace. For being able to be public about this.

[silence]

Lynette

Yeah. Telling a story that I think deserves to be heard.

[silence]

Lynette

Yeah. I don't know. Coming from the perspective of somebody left behind, right? Having gone through that, you will never put somebody else through it. I think that's motivation enough to try to fight on a bit.

[silence]

MK

Want to talk a little bit about the pain that you're feeling now?

[silence]

Lynette

It's not constant, like it used to be. It's more of triggers. Triggers, memories, wistfulness at missed events. That you just rue.

[silence]

Lynette

Honestly, for the longest time, I thought that would just mean that this is a pain that I would carry for the rest of my life. But I guess, especially over the last year since getting more plugged into the mental health space, I've learnt that you can still always carry it with you. Not hurting doesn't mean that you've forgotten, it doesn't mean that you've downplayed whatever has happened, it doesn't mean that you've—and I hate to say it—moved on.

It's more of finding a way for it to shape you as a person. For me it has directly contributed to what I want to do career-wise. And maybe that's also part of the grieving process. That's how I make meaning out of the worst possible situation.

[silence]

Lynette

Yeah. I mean on a day-to-day basis, it's not jarring or constant as it previously was. It's simpler. It's a . . .

[silence]

Lynette

It's almost optimistic. Because you're just trying to find whatever good that can come out of it. Be it a story, a motivation for what to do, other life circumstances that my friend had gone through. Yeah.

[silence]

MK

I hear you. I do.

TIME DOES NOT HEAL ALL WOUNDS

MK

Time doesn't really heal all wounds.

Lynette

They're like scars, right?

MK

Yeah.

Lynette

They heal, but there's still keloids. It's still impaired, it's still stretchy, still a bit hard to move, that kind of thing. Healing doesn't mean 'restored'. Let's say you have a surgery, there's a surgical scar. Your skin is not going to be completely like it was before. But it has healed, it has closed up, and it's still functional in a different way and you find a new way to live.

Si Qi

We had a webinar with Samaritans of Singapore and we talked about some misconceptions about suicide. For many people who attempted suicide, one of the things that they would feel is that it's okay to commit suicide because the people around them would eventually move on. It's a misconception because people never really move on.

Lynette

Yeah, yeah. Another thought is that by committing suicide, I will make the lives of the people around me better because they no longer have to deal with me being moody or me being angry at them all the time or being difficult, or whatever. Being a burden to them. Functionally, sure. But emotionally, that's absolutely not the case.

ASKING, LISTENING, AND WHAT NEXT?

Si Qi

In one of the artworks we did, it was called 'Under the Sky', we got five strangers to lie down under the sky and have conversations about mental health. I distinctly remember one of the ladies mentioning that when we ask 'How are you?' to people, the standard answer is 'I'm fine, thank you, and you?' You rarely hear people say, 'I'm having a bad day'. And even if they do say that, people tend to want to move on quickly.

As you said, being open is very difficult, even though it's necessary. And even though the immediate place where we can get help is from our immediate circle, I think there's a lot more work we have to do to learn, as you said, the kinds of questions and responses we can have to encourage openness.

How do you think the average person can start having these conversations?

Lynette

I remember when I was on exchange and I joined a school church group. What struck me the most was that they would ask 'How are you?' each week I met them, and the next week they would ask about whatever I said the previous week.

It was something so mundane, just some canned answer I gave. But next week, the same person who spoke to me the previous week would remember what I said the previous week and ask specifically about that thing again. It gives you the sense that you're really being listened to.

So asking is one thing. We talk a lot about asking, being open to asking people about how you're feeling. Maybe there needs to be more emphasis on listening to their answers. Being genuinely interested in people. Being generous with people in terms of time for them, headspace for them. We're a pretty time-bound society, I guess.

Si Qi

Fast-paced.

Lynette

Fast-paced, but also, if I'm giving you this half an hour, you only have this half an hour.

[laughter]

Lynette

Versus not having a conversation end when time is up but when the conversation has run its course or when both sides have gotten whatever they want out of it, have benefitted and are satisfied with the conversation.

I think we are moving from a society that was previously very good at listening, very good at taking orders, to a . . . I don't know if it's a society or a generation that just wants to talk all the time. Maybe it's from social media, right?

MK

Yeah.

Lynette

So we've gone from purely listening, to purely talking.

MK

I'm not sure about that though. To say that we actually purely listen, I think that's quite an overstatement because a lot of the issues that we face today are an amalgamation of the things that we haven't sorted out as a collective. So if we did listen, we wouldn't be where we're at today. And if we did listen, then that is supposed to be transferable or should be teachable.

Lynette

So where I was going with purely listening was also the not speaking part, being afraid to voice opinions. We're just . . . silent. Don't know whether we're actually listening or not, but we're not talking. And also being comfortable enough to ask for what we want. That's also another balance from demanding everything and expecting to get it, to saying: 'This is what I would like, this is what I need'. How can we find a way towards that?

Si Qi

And I think you know as you said, a part of it is being explicit in the way you love and care for other people, but the other part of the equation is being there for yourself, right? To say, 'What are my expectations for myself? What is it that I truly want for myself? If I were to put aside all the societal expectations of me, who am I really and what do I really want?' Those questions need to be answered so that we can be whole as people.

Lynette

And being okay with not having the answer immediately. I think people do ask, especially after working for a couple of years right, like 'Is this it? Is my life just going to be this . . . nine-to-five, get promoted, kind of thing? Travel over the holidays, like what else is there?' And it doesn't have to be. It also doesn't have to be some big, grand goal that you want to do and decide in your life when you're in your twenties or whatever, right?

Maybe it starts with that reflection and understanding of yourself as a person, like you said. Who you are, personality-wise, values-wise, and then I guess not compromising on that. Who can you make a difference to and what kind of difference can you make to people every day? If you're on the train, and let's say, you're a very nice person and you buy tissue from the auntie or the uncle there every day, do you just drop the money and take it or do you stop to have a conversation with them?

MK

Do you even bother looking into their eyes?

Lynette

Yeah. It's small things like that. Maybe it's recognizing the humanity in other people.

MK

That they too are fighting their own battles. Well, no matter what your socio-economic status is, how many achievements you have, it doesn't cut. You're still a human being. You come into this world by yourself, you're going to leave this world all by yourself. And if you're not really being a human being, then what are you?

WHEN WHAT YOU HAVE DOES NOT FILL UP THE HOLE OF WHAT YOU DON'T HAVE

Lynette

I was thinking about the socio-economic bit and how, some of the things that we heard in the aftermath of the suicide was like—oh but family's fairly well-to-do, well-educated, has a job, boyfriend, whatever right. *So why?* What reason does this person have to commit suicide, then?

MK

What you have doesn't fill up the hole of what you don't have. And a lot of times we forget about that. We think it's directly proportional.

Lynette

Yeah.

MK

That same level of emptiness that you felt when you were thirty-five years old could be no different from the same level of emptiness that you felt when you were fifteen.

Lynette

That's a horrible thought, but okay. Haha!

[laughter]

MK

But it's true. As we live in this material world, we subscribe to all these belief systems that we need to have this and that to be happy. You need to have a car, you need to have a family, you need to get married, you need to have a condo, you know that kind of stuff. But really? If that's really the case, how come the rich also have their problems? How come the poor also have their problems? How come the middle class also have their problems? Tells you that the material things don't really solve our problems, right?

[silence]

MK

I mean, money would allow you to hire the best psychologists, psychiatrists, doctors, all that.

Lynette

To a certain extent, yes, assuming there is that option. So everything else is equal, assuming money is the only difference, then access to resources is the difference. So what we can do and what we're trying to do, what we should do on a societal level is about how can we level that access at least. We talk about basic healthcare as an international standard goal of human rights. Basic mental healthcare should be part of that equation.

Si Qi

I think that's extremely difficult because there are so many stigmas in our society today about feeling, or feelings. Like if you're stressed, you gotta just do it.

Lynette

Suck it up.

Si Qi

Suck it up, just suck thumb[3] and continue doing it. We hear things like 'If you're sad, it will go away. Things come and go, it's okay'. But we don't really know the impact of all these seemingly insignificant things.

And maybe the problem with mental health is that sometimes it's so invisible that it's hard to point out, even to the individual. It's hard to say, *what's wrong with me? Why do I feel this way? What am I feeling?* Because feelings are complex. You think you're feeling sad but in reality, you're feeling a bunch of things— anger, disappointment, regret, altogether. But we don't have the vocabulary to express it, so there is a lot of education that needs to be done and it's truly, truly not easy.

---

[3] Just suck thumb: Singapore slang for just suck it up

Lynette

Exactly what you said about having the vocabulary. So the hardest question so far was *how are you feeling?*

[laughter]

MK

Exactly.

Lynette

We don't have the vocabulary or comfort level to answer that. When you talk about whatever you're feeling, our instinct maybe is for ourselves to say it's okay. This phrase 'It's okay' is . . .

MK

It gets on my nerves because people think that it's normal. And you're supposed to be okay. If you're not okay, you have a problem. And if you have a problem, that is also a problem. Therefore, you have to be okay. It's pretty mind-boggling if you think about it.

Lynette

Yeah. That phrase is very . . .

MK

The problem is we don't even understand our emotions in the first place. We don't even understand that we can experience conflicting feelings and emotions all in a single moment.

Lynette

And we also think that we should feel a certain way about a certain incident and if we don't, something is wrong with us.

MK

And people judge you. 'It's time to feel sad, why are you not feeling sad?'

Lynette

Yeah, pretty much.

MK

So where do we go?

[silence]

Lynette

I come back to openness. Maybe just from an individual level, being open to share stories, share the honest answers about how you're feeling, listening to whatever answers people have allowed themselves to be vulnerable enough to share, or try to, and gradually get better at it. It's not something that you get straight away. But it does get easier. So that's on an individual level.

[silence]

Lynette

I don't want to go into something like, as a whole society we should have a top-down kind of thing. I think this needs to be an active decision to be more open in our own personal lives. It's how we build culture. And I think it's culture that we should build, but also cannot prescribe.

So what we can do in our own sphere of influence, whoever we interact with, whoever, whichever paths we cross, is to reflect that attitude of openness on those few fronts.

[Background noise: Yeah!!]

MK

You heard that?

Lynette

No, I didn't!

MK

Yeah!!

[laughter]

MK

That was quite timely. Thank you.

Lynette

No, thank you.

ARE YOU GAME?

MK

It was a privilege spending my Tuesday afternoon with you.

Lynette

It's a privilege for me as well. You really never know what stuff comes up when you let yourself be open.

MK

I'm really glad that I was here.

Lynette

I'm glad you guys came down. I never thought, heck even last month or probably before you guys even emailed, I never thought I would talk about this.

And so the thing is that it always goes back to Alina, right? One of the movies that we watched together in class, it was some French movie, I think the English title was *Love Me If You Dare*. So there was a French phrase in that movie, don't know whether you guys speak French, but I don't, so my mangled version of it is, *cap ou pas cap*. Basically, 'Are you game or not?'

The movie is about these two kids just daring themselves to do stuff. I included this story in my eulogy because in school we were also daring each other to do random pranks. Each time I feel fear but also know that I need to do something, I just imagine Alina asking me that. So when I was asked to give her eulogy, the question came up, *are you game or not?* And today is another example for me. I can definitely say that each time that question has come up in my head, I have not regretted daring.

MK

Thank you for choosing to be courageous. Thank you for choosing courage all the time.

Lynette

I try.

MK

It takes courage to choose courage, if you understand what I mean. Thank you. I'm glad that we crossed paths.

CHAPTER 2

Sometimes Love is Just Not Enough

By Adrian Pang, Actor, Artistic Director, Pangdemonium Theatre Company

Adrian experienced depressive episodes throughout his life, but it was not until Circuit Breaker[4] in March 2020 when his family gave him a firm nudge to see a therapist that he started working on his mental health. Adrian shares his personal struggles with mental health, and reflects on the thought that 'sometimes love is not enough'. While we can care and love the people around us deeply, sometimes professional mental health help is needed, and there should be no shame in seeking mental healthcare treatment.

---

[4] Circuit Breaker refers to the three month nationwide lockdown in Singapore to curb the spread of COVID-19

EVERYTHING WAS WELL. BUT I WASN'T.

MK

Could you share with us your own journey of understanding and working on your mental health?

Adrian

I think what I've realized recently is that from a very early age, and when I say early age, I mean my mid-teens or even earlier. Thinking about it now, I've had an inclination towards being very insular, but also kind of burying myself in this hole full of darkness.

It's only with a bit of hindsight now that I can identify certain points in my life where I just go through these long periods of feeling very down. That's how I can look at it now. But as I went into my late teens, early adult life, I think the first significant period of my life where I had found myself in a very dark place was during my National Service (NS)[5] days. I was very isolated from a lot of people. I didn't want to talk to anybody. I kind of alienated myself from my friends. I felt very alone. It sounds like typical angsty young man type of thing, but when I look back now, I can safely identify that as a long, protracted depressive episode I couldn't get out of.

And then you know, eventually when I started working as an actor, I would find myself going through periods of feeling extremely down and lost as well, which is not uncommon when you're freelancing as an actor. You're just going from job to job, you go through periods of unemployment, and you just question your own worth, all that kind of stuff. It just goes with the territory. But I suppose most recently what was significant was that despite everything seemingly going well for myself, there were periods

---

[5] National Service: Compulsory service in the uniformed services in Singapore

where I felt completely hopeless and helpless, and was not able to pick myself up.

But five years ago, my older son, Zack, at that time he was about sixteen or so, he was going through a difficult period. We were all aware of it in the family. We rallied around him to support him, and it became apparent very quickly that that wasn't enough. And oh God, strangely enough, it was Zack going to his younger brother, Xander, who is a year younger, to basically say *I need help*. When I think about it now, it kind of breaks my heart because even though we've always had a very open relationship with our boys, very open communication, the two brothers are so, *so* close. Our boys share a closeness with each other that even us as parents don't share with them.

And so Xander came to us eventually and said 'Listen, Zack told me that he's really in a desperate state and he really needs help'. I was like *oh god! This is really beyond anything that I thought it would be.* I thought just giving him extra TLC would . . . slowly usher him out of this. But obviously that's not enough. And it broke my heart because as a parent, I felt totally helpless. I felt I was failing my son.

We went to Zack and said 'Your brother says that you really need help and we're here to offer you any kind of help that you need'. Gosh, I can remember this image of him just not being able to get out of bed and us just going, 'Don't worry, we're fully behind this, we will find help for you'.

So we went and sought a counsellor for him. Zack went to see the counsellor first, and after that, the counsellor invited me in. And God, you know, when I started talking, I suddenly found myself in tears. All the stuff from forty years ago just all started coming out. But that was the first step in Zack's journey and he very quickly managed to pull himself out of that hole. So we're all very relieved about that and since then, he's been on a very even keel and he's been absolutely fine. He's very happy now at drama school.

SPIRALING DOWN, DOWN, DOWN . . .

Adrian

Then two years later, I found myself in a hole for my own stupid reasons. Just questioning myself and what I was doing with my life and my worth and all that kind of stuff. I seem to go through these cycles.

MK

How old were you when this happened?

Adrian

This was 2018, so this is three years ago now, I was fifty-two. I was in a really *really* low place and I happened to be rehearsing for a play that was all out, balls-to-the-wall comedy, very physical, very over the top, and *oh God*, the energy was just sapped out of me every day because I was feeling at my lowest. But at the same time, on stage, I had to put on this mask of pretending I was at my highest and it just really sapped away my energy.

I remember moments during the day when I'd be halfway through rehearsal and I would just suddenly stare off into the distance and Tracy, my wife and director, would notice and she would have to pat me and just snap me back to reality. I was just staring into nothingness and feeling empty and terrible. Terrible! But that period, with the patience and the care of my family, they guided me through that period, and I found a way to pick myself up again.

And then last year, when COVID became a thing, nobody expected it to last this long. When it first started, we thought we'd be okay in a couple of months. We were running our own theatre company of fifteen staff, trying to motivate everybody, trying to instill some sense of optimism. We were also reaching out to people in the theatre community to ask how they were just to make sure everybody's okay, and that we're all in this together, all these kinds of things.

But then very quickly, by mid-March, I found myself slipping into this—I keep on using this word—this hole of darkness again and I just went further and further and deeper and deeper. By April and May, I just couldn't get out of bed. I couldn't sleep for one thing. I would be coming down the stairs in the morning just to get a drink, watch something on TV just to hopefully lull myself into a sleep. I was watching the terrible crap on Netflix and getting really emotional, and I was like, *Why am I crying? This is a zombie movie! And I'm crying? What the hell!* And then I couldn't go to sleep. And next morning when it's time to wake up, cannot wake up, cannot get out of bed. Just feeling heavy. Heavy-hearted. Heavy in my head. Heavy body. Just catatonic, almost. And taking long walks in the rain, crying in the rain. Very drama.

[laughter]

Adrian

And I was just in a stupor. I realize that had largely to do with the fact that the pandemic had kind of rendered me, once again, questioning my worth, my value, my purpose and my meaning in life.

I run a theatre company, I'm an actor, and I can't do my job anymore. If I can't do my job, what the hell am I? What's the point of me? That kind of thing. And it lasted almost four months. During that time, I tried, in my own way, to take care of myself. I started an exercise regime. I started to wake up in the morning and meditate for ten minutes, whatever meditation means, because I never really bought into that but it's just a bit of quiet time to myself every morning in bed before I actually get out of it, before I even look at my phone. Then I would come downstairs, *sayang*[6] my cat, have a nice breakfast, listen to some chill music before I start the day and open the laptop. That kind of helped, to have some kind of a routine, a bit of exercise.

My wife, bless her, she used to take me out on rides on her Vespa to the beach. During the Circuit Breaker, when we were all imprisoned in our homes anyway, we were allowed to go and get some fresh air. We would hop on the bike, go to the beach, just walk a little bit. And even then, I remember occasions when we would get there and I would just sit there very, very quietly and she would just sit there, not even having to talk. Because I just didn't have the energy to talk. But that was just getting through the day and living day by day and surviving, really.

THE FINAL STRAW

Adrian

It just got to a point where the family decided to give me a firm nudge to seek professional help. I realized that at Pangdemonium[7], we've staged several productions over the years that deal with mental health.

[silence]

Adrian

I always speak to the audience at the end of the show. I would invariably say that mental health and mental illnesses are real. They are all around us in our community much more than we realize. There are many more people around us who are living with some form of mental illness than we care to think about, and that if you know anybody or if you yourself are living with something, please go and talk to someone professional. It's not shameful to talk to

---

[6] Sayang: Malay word meaning 'to love'

[7] Pangdemonium: Adrian's theatre company

someone, it's an act of courage to seek help. I always say this. I sing this song at every show that we do.

In fact, the last show that we did before lockdown was a play called *The Son*, where I played the father of a teenager who was going through depression. I played a father who was very intractable, who didn't want to understand or even accept that his son was suffering through this. And ironically two months later, there I was in that situation of my depression.

So my family encouraged me to go and seek help and I finally relented. I went straight to my GP and said, 'Listen, I'm desperate, I've been in this darkness for the last three and a half months, I need help. I will go see a counsellor, I've already made an appointment, but is there any kind of medication that you can give me?' And it's strange because he looked at me and went, 'Oh really? How bad is it? Can't you, I don't know, do anything like, exercise?' I said, 'I already did that' and even as we were having this conversation, it became very clear to me that not everybody buys into the reality of it, even a medical professional. They . . .

[silence]

Adrian

It just highlighted to me what a stigma mental health and mental illness still is.

So I said, 'I've tried all that, but I've come to you to ask if you can recommend me to someone who can prescribe something'. And he said, 'Well actually, I can prescribe you something'. I said 'Please, whatever it is you can do, just to kickstart me on this recovery journey'. And he said, 'Yeah okay, okay, I'll put you on the lowest dose of this thing, but it doesn't work straightaway'. I said 'I know, I'm just willing to try anything'. I was that desperate. So he gave me a course of escitalopram for . . . a month first? Or three months. So I started on that, and as expected, it wasn't an overnight thing, and it took me maybe about three weeks before I started to, literally I remember the feeling of waking up one morning and going like, *Eh, I don't feel like death anymore. I think I can get out of bed! Oh oh, meditate first.* At three weeks it just suddenly decided, *okay lah, give you lah, give you a good feeling.*

Along with that, I started seeing my counsellor, wonderful lady. At first it started on Zoom. Oh my god, crying over Zoom is quite an experience. For two hours, sitting there, crying into your screen [laughter]. So, the first two sessions were on Zoom and then Circuit Breaker lifted and I started to go and see her every week in person because it was only then that mental health professionals I think, were eventually deemed to be essential workers. It was another case of, *wow, people really don't take this seriously.* So those continued for weeks and weeks and weeks and I found myself feeling better and better and better until the sessions were just me talking about my day and her giving me some self-care tools to help me when I was feeling down again, to help me deal with anxiety because I also realized in this whole journey that part of my depressive tendency was also anxiety.

So, it's been more than nine months already since then and it's gone by like that. The COVID situation has improved, slightly. There's vaccination. Theatre has reopened a little bit. I'm able to go back to work, I've been filming the last few months. That whole sense once again of purpose and of worth and of meaning and all that in a very tangible form has come back. But I think much more importantly, I'm just dealing with day-to-day life a lot better.

It's strange, I think. Maybe it's a partly psychosomatic or a purely psychological thing of *okay, I'm on an upward journey, I'm on meds that are helping me modulate my moods.* Whenever I encounter an event or incident that can trigger me to become really down or angry, I take a moment literally to just take a breath and distance myself from it a little bit and go, *you have a choice.* You could react that way and everybody becomes miserable, or you could react in a very much more controlled way. Which one has better repercussions? And most of the time, I think 90 per cent of the time, I choose the latter and I deal with it.

But it's going to be a lifetime journey, I think. I know that it's not something that's been totally fixed and I can, you know, neglect self-care. Of course, I wondered whether I would dare to go off my medication, but I think I'll stick with it for now.

So talking about medication is by no means me saying that the moment you're feeling down, go and take prescription meds straight away because I think that's quite a dangerous thing to advocate. I'm just speaking personally, that it works for me. But go and seek help. Speak to a mental health professional and get a definitive diagnosis and take it seriously. *Take it seriously.* I've become much more aware of young people like yourselves being much more open to talking about it. It's still a stigma, I mean the show that we did last year, *The Son*, so many people who came to see the show wrote to us afterwards and said, 'Thank you for staging this play'. A lot of young people said 'This is exactly what I've been going through for years. Nobody understands and this play has told my story and it just makes me feel less alone, less of a freak, and I brought some friends and even they now understand me better'.

One lady who I've been in touch with for the last year and a half, wrote to me after she came to see the show with her daughter, to tell me that her daughter has been going through exactly the same thing. Self-harming for some years now. And she said that halfway through the play, her daughter actually reached over and said to her, 'Mum, this is me. You know that this is me'. But on the other hand, halfway through the play, her husband said 'Why you drag me to this show? It's so depressing'. And the mum said 'Exactly, you work all day, you don't see, this is what I deal with, with our daughter. You don't see it, you don't want to see it, but this is what she's going through, what we're going through as a family'.

Some of this is so personal and private. It's such a private pain that you just don't know whether you can talk to anybody to even explain how you feel. That's the crux of it. You have a physical pain, you can say 'It's here, this is where it hurts. My leg hurts. My arm hurts. This is exactly where it hurts. Please take me to the doctor,' and chances are, your family says 'Okay yeah it hurts you, I can't cure it, I'll take you to the doctor'. Whereas if it's a psychological, mental or even an emotional issue, chances are your parents' nurturing instincts will try to sayang the pain away, love it away. But love . . . And this was a line in the play we did: *sometimes love is just not enough*. And that's so true! You think that you love your children and that will solve all their problems but when your child is suffering a hurt of the mind, a hurt of the heart, if you will, you can support them all you want, and of course love them, support them, make them feel that you are there for them, but you can't cure them. You have to take them to a professional just like you would if you were suffering from a broken arm, a tumour, or something. You can't love a tumour away. You can't love cancer away. You can only hope that a medical professional can help them. So similar to that, a mental illness has to be treated as an illness that needs professional help. I'm at the age of fifty-five and going through my own journey, only I'm so late in the game, realizing for myself that it's a real thing. So that's why any chance for me to make some noise about it, I will. So yeah. That's your whole chapter already.

No need to ask any more questions. Thank you very much, and goodnight.

[laughter]

Adrian

Yeah, like that, you ask one question and I talk for half an hour.

[laughter]

WHO THE HELL TOOK MY GLASS?!

MK

What are you connected to as you're sharing that?

Adrian

What am I connected to? God, I'm amazed that I can even now talk about it now without getting overly emotional.

There was a period when every time I had to speak about this, and because I was still right in the midst of it, I would get very emotional. And I'm not saying that I'm out of the woods by any means, because I could still be very easily triggered by something, and I know that on a daily basis, something will confront me and I could very well slip into it again. But I think strangely enough, this COVID thing has given me a different perspective of myself and my life and . . . I guess, I've just been trying to be a little bit more philosophical about things. And also, I think a sense of gratitude. I mean there's that whole saying that the key to happiness is thankfulness, *that thing*.

[laughter]

Adrian

I think I'm buying into that more and more nowadays. Just being thankful because I think it's so easy to say that the glass is half empty. And I've always said that for me, it's not even about whether the glass is full or empty. It's like, *who the hell took my glass?!* That's me. Or *eh, how come my glass is broken?*

But I have a glass and it may be only partly filled but I'm grateful for what I have, because it's good. I guess I've always been afraid of being complacent. And that's why I always feel that I'm not enough or I haven't done enough, and that's why I need to keep on doing more and working harder, and striving for more so that I feel that I have served a purpose. So that I feel that I have lived a worthwhile life. Because I mean, that comes with the territory of low self-esteem and insecurity and . . . Feeling like I am not worthwhile, that kind of stuff.

MK

Did you notice it?

Adrian

Sorry, what?

MK

Did you notice that you just brushed it off again?

Adrian

Yeah, I did, I did! It's a thing, it's a thing. Because I know that's how I am. I think I always have been like this. It's part of my upbringing, it's part of my DNA. Maybe it's just being Asian.

MK

Is your dad still around?

Adrian

Yeah, my parents are still around. It's that kind of clichéd story of whether I've done my parents proud, whether I've done enough to justify all the sacrifices that they made, and feeling guilt.

Guilt is a huge motivator in my life. Like I said, it's a very clichéd Singaporean, Asian, burden that I bear. That's why I guess I've tried to, as much as I can, not inflict that on my two sons as well and let them follow their own path and create their own journey through life. But you know, having made the choices that I made in my work, I've tried to reconcile myself with it. Not to say that my parents are not supportive of it, because they are, they come and see everything I do and my mum makes a big deal of it. But I don't know, I can never shake the feeling that there is some disappointment, I suppose, and there's always going to be something I can't make up to my parents for. So, it doesn't help.

I'm not blaming them by any means. My parents are wonderful, I love them. But I guess there will always be that feeling of, I wish I could have made them *prouder*, all that kind of stuff. That feeling doesn't . . . doesn't help.

MK

Doesn't disappear.

Adrian

Yeah, doesn't disappear. And doesn't help my own questioning of my self-worth and tendencies towards depression and all that kind of stuff. But you just deal with it lah I mean. I'm not an isolated case, I'm not a special case by any means. I'm sure a lot of people identify with this.

MK

If you could have turned back time, what would you have done differently?

Adrian

If I could have, done anything differently? I don't think . . .

[silence]

Adrian

I really don't know.

[silence]

Adrian

It's strange. If you were to ask me this two years ago, five years ago . . . Now, I'm in a very strange place where I'm able to actually say, *You know, my life has worked out the way it has simply because of all the things that I've been through and the journey that I've been through, and I'm grateful.*

I have a lot of people in my life who have been significant in my journey, people who are proud of the work that I do. Sure, there'll always be a sense of wanting more, there'll always be a sense of envy, which is a terrible thing, it's such a toxic thing. A sense of, *have I done enough?* And you know now that my two boys are at the cusp of going to the next stage of their lives, possibly leaving the home. That's another life-changing thing for me as well.

In a parallel universe I might have become a lawyer but . . .

[laughter]

Adrian

Oh man, I can't even imagine that.

[laughter]

Adrian

Here I am, I do what I do. Mm. Like that.

[laughter]

WHO IS ADRIAN PANG?

Si Qi

I wanted to ask . . . I don't know if it's too personal to ask this.

I think people see Adrian Pang as The Adrian Pang who's on stage, who's on screen, who has a lot going on—Pangdemonium, a great family, a great career, and beautiful house as well.

These are the things that the average person strives for. Love, family, career, some material things like a house or a car, things that seem to be the precursor to happiness, the precursor to whatever thing that they think should do next. Like *I need all this before I can embark on my passions,* or whatever.

Perhaps people think that you have it all. But it's . . . you're still struggling with self-worth and things like that. So what is it that all this doesn't fill?

Adrian

I mean. This kind of material stuff I guess has been a by-product of working hard and I'm very lucky. As I said before, the fact that I am pursuing something I LOVE, with a *passion*, as my career is something that I'm very fortunate and privileged to be able to do. I mean it's a priceless thing in a way. And the fact that I've been able to pursue that and take care of my family and afford certain things is a bonus. But I don't think we can reverse engineer it that way to say that I've got all the material things, that's why I'm happy.

If I were to lose all these material things, yeah, I'd be a little bit pissed off.

[laughter]

Adrian

But I'd still have the family. I think. I would hope.

[laughter]

Adrian

And that's also priceless. But you know, the fact that I've been doing what I do for thirty years now is something that I don't take for granted. Because not everybody can say that. I know a lot of people who hate their jobs and are earning tons of cash. You're cash-rich but you're otherwise, spiritually destitute. Not to say that they're destitute, I'm sure they've found ways to be happy as well, but I guess it's just balancing out what matters in life.

For me, I decided to be an actor knowing that all I wanted to do was to act and to work and just keep on working. And if

I would be able to just keep doing that for the rest of my life, paying rent and feeding myself, I'd be okay. That's why in my own journey to where I am now, I have to look back and just be thankful that I managed to do this. But everyone's journey is different.

That's why I brought up the thing about envy. Once you start comparing yourself with somebody else, you're bound to feel bad about yourself. There's always somebody else who's doing better than you, who's luckier than you, and that whole element of, *why does that person get that, I've been working my ass off and I—*

Si Qi

I think it happens a lot in the entertainment industry.

Adrian

Oh, I'm sure. And it's so poisonous. It can drag you down and make you feel even more worthless and make you always look at the other way because the grass is always greener—

MK

On the other side.

Adrian

And that whole thing is a real killer because it can make you feel bitter, jaded, and cynical and make you feel bad about your own work and your own worth. I've seen it happen to colleagues of mine, and it's always knocking on my own door. So I'm always trying to stave it off and keep the wolf from the door. And at the same time, just trying to look at what I have and go *it's good, it's good, it's good.* Not in a self-satisfied kind of manner but just to say *do not diminish yourself, do not diminish your own achievements.*

Because for me, as an actor, it's a very self-absorbed, self-indulgent occupation, literally for an occupation. It's all about *me me me.* I do what I do because I want you to *LOVE* me, I want you to *adore* me, I want you to think that I'm *great.*

That's the crux of being an actor. But I've tried to balance that out by very sincerely and genuinely doing work and creating, especially though Pangdemonium, work that I hope speaks to people. That is my way of providing some kind of service, if you'd like, to my fellow men, to the community, not just as entertainment but food for the soul and food for the heart, and food for the mind. And if I'm able to just touch one person out of 600 people in one sitting in a meaningful, personal way that makes them want to take positive action or feel better about themselves or want to make a change in themselves, then I suppose I feel a bit better about the self-involved, self-absorbent nature of my work.

[It starts to rain at the outdoor patio]

Adrian

I've young emerging actors who come to me and ask for advice. And I usually hate to give advice. But lately I think I've worked it out in my head, what it is that drives me.

I always tell them, do pursue this only if it's the *only, only, only, only* one thing in your life that you feel that you can do and want to do, because if there's anything else in your life that you are good at, that you enjoy doing, that you can make a decent enough living doing, and you serve some kind of useful purpose to the community—if you can tick these four boxes, anything else in your life that ticks these four boxes, please go and do that instead.

MK

Ikigai.

Adrian

What's that?

Si Qi

Ikigai. You know?

MK

The Japanese model.

Adrian

Ah? What?

MK

Exactly the same four factors that you're talking about.

Adrian

Are you kidding? What, who? I didn't even know this. Ikigai?

Si Qi

Yeah so, I can't really recall what it is, but at the centre, it overlaps. So if your purpose and how you make your money and your passion can fold together, then that is your Ikigai.

MK

Correct. So it's a Venn diagram. Those four things that you spoke about. And you're talking about the centre of it where these four actually meet.

Adrian

Ikigai? Okay, see this is new. I thought I was being terribly original and clever but no, bloody Ikigai. Wait, is Ikigai the name of a person?

MK

It's a framework.

Adrian

Oh, it's a model, is it? Wow, okay. I must look it up. Wow. Okay I thought I copyrighted the thing but it's been done. I'll look it up. But yeah I mean.

[laughter]

Adrian

Actors are forever stealing inspiration from other people and thinking it's their own but yeah, I guess I recently bought into this theory.

Si Qi

You just had your 'We Can Achieve' moment.

Adrian

Yeah!

[laughter]

Adrian

Exactly, I know, I know, I know, oh God. I'm just full of clichés. So I've been telling these young people and they're going *wooooah*, but they're probably going, *oh Ikigai lah, doesn't this guy know anything?*

[laughter]

Adrian

But yeah, it's true. So if you can't tick these four boxes while pursuing a career in the arts or whatever, then don't. If there's something else that fulfils all that, do that instead because this life is going to beat you down. 99 per cent of us you know, just turn out to be weirdos.

[laughter]

SNAP OUT OF IT

Si Qi

So, you mentioned that you've been kind of feeling down since you were fifteen or even before that. So on the topic of mental health stigmas, what stopped you from getting help?

Adrian

I think it was just telling myself that it was just a passing phase and I would find a way to pull myself out of it, or snap out of it. Just busying myself with daily stuff and nonsense to either distract myself or to hang onto and say *this will make me feel better*. Just keep working, keep working, keep working. Just deny lah, just denying, denying, denying to myself.

It's so easy to do that, to push it aside. And then you find yourself not feeling that way anymore. Just not seeing that it wasn't just a sporadic incidental occasional spectre that would come and visit me. This spectre was always looming around, casting a shadow over me.

I think I've reconciled with myself that it's very likely that this presence in my life will probably be with me for the rest of my life. I think I've just kind of learnt to maybe make friends with him, and hopefully be the one in control of him rather than him controlling me. I'm learning to do that. Who knows? I may slip again. It could take just the slightest thing for me to lose my footing and find myself plunging into that hole once again and him kind of coming up to pull me down. Who knows? God help me if that does happen, but for now, as we're talking here on 24 March 2021, I am balancing it all out.

Last night, something happened which made me feel a little bit *urghhh*. It took me a few hours to calm myself down and tell myself that *there's a way to deal with this, there's a way to deal with this, there's a way to deal with this that doesn't make you fly off the rails*. Just talking to myself. It's a very conscious, active process actually, rather than just letting it be. So rather than just letting it take its course, it's almost a physical exercise to control it. If you will.

Si Qi

It's okay not to be okay, until it isn't.

Adrian

Yeah, exactly! That's the thing, because before you know that you're not okay, you're so not okay until sometimes you cannot even help yourself anymore which is where I found myself. So, um. Yeah. It's a daily thing.

MK

What do you think we can do from an individual to a collective level besides just advocating, besides just talking out about mental health, to raise more awareness about this issue?

Adrian

I think education in schools, for one thing, is very key. I'm not aware of whether they talk about this in schools now, but certainly not in my school days. But I think it should start from primary school level, and definitely from secondary school level.

I really think something's got to be done with that because that will be a huge step towards hopefully breaking the stigma. Because you know how Singaporean parents are like. Once you put it into the school curriculum, it becomes a real thing. But I think education is key. Educating parents, for one. But I don't know where you'd start with that because a lot of parents don't want to know. Adults don't want to know. *How dare you tell me how to look after my kids?*

That's why hopefully, through whatever small ways myself and people like me talk about it, being as open as I can about it, about sharing my own experience, hopefully somebody will pay attention. Somebody will listen and go *that's how I feel as well* and hopefully that motivates them to do something. But the conversation is starting and strangely enough this is a conversation that I've been having on many occasions in the past year. So you know, people are starting to want to talk about it and I know young people are much more open to talking about it.

This whole self-care thing is very important. I think we need to encourage that, especially in a time right now when we can all become so absorbed with just restarting businesses, and yet we haven't started with our own housekeeping.

MK

Adrian, I have a question, but this question is optional, just something that is coming out in my space.

[silence]

MK

How did you cope when you had thoughts of dying?

Adrian

Um.

MK

. . . That's a very bad question.

Adrian

No, it's very strange, because what kind of surprised me was that it was such an easy thing to think about.

It's strange to think about it now as I'm talking about it to you guys, but those occasions where the idea of dying, of death, or whatever crossed my mind, it wasn't even with any sense of fear, any sense of dread, or sense of *oh, better not*. It was just almost a frighteningly easy thing to think about, because when you're in a mental and emotional state of numbness, even a thought as extreme as death doesn't even scare you. And it scares me now to think about how not scary it was. But back then, I remember lying in bed and going *God if I just disappear now, if I just cease to exist now, so what?* And it's so frightening to think that the mind can trick you into even thinking that. And just, wow.

I mean now, I shiver at the thought, obviously. So I just think about what I would be giving up. Think about the life that I have, people that I have around me. But it was just a fleeting thought that popped into my head, and luckily it went away. I wouldn't have done anything. But I know people who have. I dread to think how they're feeling when they're actually doing it. But yeah. I never thought I would get to a point in my life where that would even occur to me. But it has.

But here I am. Ikigai. Ikigai. Ikigai.

MK

I-k-i-g-a-i.

JUST ADRIAN PANG

Si Qi

So I think roles and identities are a thing that a lot of people struggle with. All of us play a lot of different roles in our lives, be it husband, father, son, employee, friend, the spectrum. And it's not easy to manage all of that and the expectations that come with it. And I think you have an interesting layer on top of it, being an actor, playing then another spectrum of roles. What is it like to manage these different roles in your line?

Adrian

Actually, I used to see it as a way to pretend to be not me, as an escape. Cause I mean, if you're someone who doesn't like themselves very much in the first place, I have the perfect job for that. Because I get to pretend to be other people.

But I think subconsciously in the last ten years perhaps, ironically since we started Pangdemonium, it's just the stories that we tell. If I'm involved in the production in any way, if I'm playing a role in it, subconsciously I've started to use these stories and these roles as a means of understanding myself more, reaching inside my own history and my own baggage or my own skeletons and exposing them more and more in order to channel it, to feed into the roles that I play rather than ignoring myself. To be honest, it's a very basic thing that actors do. You always invest a part of yourself in whatever role, but I think now I'm seeing more value in that, just to make these characters richer and I suppose, more authentic and more real.

So rather than running away from myself, I'm incorporating more of myself and in the process, I'm learning more about myself, for better or for worse. I'm just kind of learning and maturing as an actor as well. And I'd like to think it's making the roles that I play more interesting. Even now after thirty years, I'm still learning my craft, I'm still learning new processes and getting new tools. I hope to do this for the rest of my life as long as I'm capable of it.

[thunder claps]

Si Qi

Ominous thunder.

Adrian

(voice acting) As long as I'm capable of it, hahaha! *That's what you think, says God.*

[laughter]

MK

Last question. If there's something you want the world out there to know, what would that be? No cliché stuff, just your truth.

Adrian

I think you never really know what the next person is going through. We are so conditioned to wear masks in public all the time or even with the person closest to us. So never assume anything. And if you're going to ask that person, 'How are you?', really mean that question and be ready for that person to actually want to tell you how they are, because I think everyday interactions can be either totally meaningless or they can be your next meaningful interaction and relationship with someone.

And also, there's a line from the play, *The Son*—'Sometimes love is not enough'. If you're going through something that is out of your control, you don't have to suffer in silence. There is help, and there is no shame in seeking help because you just might save someone's life, and that life could be your own.

MK

Thank you.

Si Qi

Thank you.

Adrian

You're very welcome.

CHAPTER 3

A Positive Life Does Not Always Have Positive Emotions

By Belinda Ang, Founder, ARTO

Belinda faced many challenges in her career, first as an entrepreneur starting an F&B business in Singapore, and later as an artist and label manager in the entertainment industry. The long hours, stressful work environments, and toxic relationships she was in eventually took a toll on her mental wellness. She started having anxiety attacks, and knew it was time to see a therapist. Therapy allowed her to put a magnifying glass on her life, and understand how the things that happened to her in her childhood continued to shape who she was as an adult. She walked out finding greater self-respect and a deeper relationship with her inner child, and hopes to create a positive impact through her latest business venture, ARTO.

ART AS A VEHICLE FOR HEAVY TOPICS

MK

Could you tell me more about yourself and ARTO?

Belinda

I'm currently the CEO and founder of ARTO, a social art discovery platform, and what we want to do is make art accessible physically and emotionally and inspire 98 per cent of the world's population to consume more art. That is the overall vision and mission for us. We're in the middle of development currently, and we do hope we can start engaging with art lovers in the next one or two months. As for myself, I am almost forty, but not forty yet, haha! I have two younger siblings, and I love animals. I'm very geeky because there are days like today where I just want to stay at home. I'll prioritize my family and my animals above everything else.

[laughter]

MK

One of the things you've probably realized is that at ThisConnect, we create a lot of performative, participatory, and instructional art that discusses mental health issues, which can get very heavy when it comes to topics like depression and suicide. How do you think art can be an effective medium to create these kinds of conversations? How does art create spaces for people to have emotional connection?

Belinda

I think even among friends I know or my own social groups, I'm a bit of a dreamer. Maybe what I say would not be as easily understood by the rest of the population as well, but I do think that art is a perfect vehicle for heavy topics because there's no preaching involved. That's one. It's very different from reading the news or reading heavy articles or trying to finish a documentary. It doesn't attempt to preach or educate in a top-down approach, in a way that says *I know it better than you*. I think art allows the space and a bit of personal me-time for the audience to think about issues, and that issue would differ from person to person, so it doesn't necessarily offer answers to any question or any issue— be it talking about mental health or gender equality—but it does allow people to think about questions in a provoking way that they normally would not in a typical situation. And because it doesn't judge, because it is not a top-down educational approach, people are more willing to be vulnerable to those thoughts, because they feel it's a personal space. The fact that art presents a question, offers the space, and allows the audience to be vulnerable in their own personal boundaries—that is the most powerful thing that art does.

A PRESSURE COOKER DOESN'T EXPLODE OVERNIGHT

MK

I think one thing that's interesting is that you're a startup founder, and you've also been an entrepreneur since you were twenty-one, which is quite unconventional in Singapore. Could you tell me more about why you decided to go into entrepreneurship? How does your path relate to your personal mental health journey as well?

Belinda

In between my professional career, I have worked for companies before, but I will just touch on that as a journey and the differences it had on mental health for me personally.

Back then when I was twenty-one, I started my first food business, which lasted for about six years or so. By the time I graduated from that, I was twenty-six or twenty-seven. I didn't know what an entrepreneur was. I didn't wake up and say, *hey, I wanna be an entrepreneur.* It wasn't about that. It was more like, *hey, I'm passionate about something, I really enjoy doing this, and people said that they would pay me to do this.*

At that point in time, it was salad. It was like in 2003 or 2004, when there weren't many salad bars in Singapore yet. Back then, people would ask you why the vegetables were purple—that's how far we've come. So I was really passionate about salads and I thought I should do it myself. It wasn't because entrepreneurship was a sexy thing; no one in my family had ever run their own business. So the entire idea of entrepreneurship wasn't a conscious decision. It was more *I want to do this, so let's start doing it.* Well, when it comes to that part of my life, I think it is quite interesting, but I'm not sure if I want to do it all over again.

[laughter]

Belinda

It was stressful in its own way, as compared to my peers in my age group. A lot of the stress came from isolation because we were spending sixteen to eighteen hours a day in the kitchen. You had no friends. Even if you did have friends, whenever they asked you out to join them for dinner or KTV[8], you can never make it because your business always comes first. In an F&B business, we have no off days. It's seven days a week, and the only off-days we take are during Chinese New Year. I don't start that early. I have chefs coming in early, but I start around 1.30 p.m. all the way till 1.30 a.m., and by the time you pack up and go home and have your dinner, it's about 2 a.m. to 3 a.m. in the morning. That's my dinner time. I get a bit of me-time and I go to bed at about 5 a.m. to 6 a.m. Sometimes things happened in the kitchen and you just had to wake up at 7 a.m. to go and solve it. Over time,

---

[8] KTV: Karaoke Television

it took a toll on my health. There was a period of time when I couldn't even walk. There was also the feeling of loneliness which added its own weight. But because I have a very supportive family, it wasn't actually that tough.

I think the toughest part was when I had to give up my cafe because we were not making money, my dad met with an accident, and my boyfriend went MIA[9]. So, it was a bad breakup, I was losing my business, my dad had an accident, and I had a bank loan to pay off. I needed to cut my losses short. I think what helped me to get out that phase was just focusing purely on my priorities. It's not healthy, but it's like, I had no time for emotions, so I just had to put whatever emotions I had aside and just focus on my priorities. I realized that this method serves you okay for a while, but it's a pressure cooker. A pressure cooker's not gonna explode in one to two months, it's gonna explode in a decade. Haha! But while that lasted, that was how I got through that period. I had a couple of jobs that brought me to places. I joined two event companies and was leading the digital team in a PR firm in Singapore. I actually think I feel more stressed working with colleagues than running my own business, even if my business was doing badly. I could be paid a lot better than if I were running my own business. But working in an office environment was way more stressful for me.

The other interesting phase in my life was when I was in entertainment. Earlier in my career, I was an artist manager and label manager. I think that, mentally, that was the worst phase of my life. Downright the worst. At the end of those six years, I had to see a therapist.

[Belinda laughs]

Belinda

It was really bad. But I would say that it was the entire environment, the toxic relationships, as well as this inclination towards a

---

[9] MIA: Missing in action

codependent relationship didn't help my mental wellness. But more importantly now, when I look back at that period of time, I think it was a blessing in disguise because of how low I was. I believe I had very mild depression. I wasn't suicidal, but it was a super chronic depression that lasted for a very long time, and I was having anxiety attacks. At that point, I knew I needed help, so I went to see a therapist. I think that was one of the best decisions I made in my life. It not only allowed me to resolve the issues at hand, but it also allowed me to look at my entire life in a fast forward format with a huge magnifying glass.

I realized that there were a lot of repetitive patterns, confirmation bias, and negative beliefs. I realized that how I behaved or how I responded towards people was not something that just happened. It was something that had its roots in a certain point in my life—obviously childhood, not a surprise there. The fact is that the incident or event wasn't even traumatizing. It was just something that happened, and I formed a negative belief, and it just repeated my entire life.

We think that we need something traumatizing to actually form negative beliefs. I realized that it's not the case. It's just the cause and effect of the way we perceive certain moments in life, and if that has a negative impact, then it is a limiting belief that we formed in our lives. When we were seven or nine, whatever happened to us in that moment was huge. But now when we look back at it, we just laugh. I think too often, we laugh at our inner child and not recognize that we should listen to it. I think I became a totally changed person after that drama. Whether it was in the way I approached people and led my life or picked my priorities—everything changed.

That's why when I look back, I go, *wow, if I hadn't been through that low point, I would never have grown up.* I'm a lot closer to my inner child right now, and I care about how I feel rather than just dismiss it. I respect myself a lot more, especially when it comes to mental health of any sorts.

STAY TRUE TO YOUR WORDS

MK

You know, for many entrepreneurs, their careers are a manifestation or expression of their purpose. Having this purpose is very tightly knitted with a person's mental wellbeing. Having a purpose also gives a person meaning; if not, one can feel very lost and hopeless, especially when they're on a difficult path. How do you think purpose is tied with one's mental health and wellbeing?

Belinda

The thing is, I've never given that proper thought. I don't think I'm so noble to say that I'm doing this because there are mental health benefits, even though I know that there are.

I think that I'm still a little bit free-spirited in terms of my nature and character. It's super important to find something you enjoy so you don't wake up every day trying to kick yourself in the ass while grumbling and hating life. I personally feel that everyone's life has a fair destination. You always end with death—that's it. You were born without you saying you wanted to, and suddenly before you say *hey, I approve of dying,* you just leave. I think what is unfair or different about everyone else is the middle, which is the process. So, if you're going to die anyway—and this is totally not religious right—I'm just saying that what makes the difference is the process. You don't want to live your life doing something you hate, that's it. Very simple. Everything that I like, when opportunities are presented, what calls out to me . . . What I like is that it doesn't matter what I do—it could be F&B, music, film, marketing, or art. No matter what I'm doing, I always believe that *okay, you're doing A, but how can you further add value to the people you work with or in the world that you're living in, in very small capacities?*

You know the butterfly effect? My personal mission is to change the world, but I don't intend to be Steve Jobs or

Mother Theresa. I sincerely believe that you only need to change the course of one person to change the world. Because everything works in a domino effect, right? And if no matter what I'm doing, I'm able to do the right thing by every individual I come across, I think and sincerely believe there will be a positive snowball effect. And I hope it gets paid forward, because I'm also the beneficiary of a lot of good people, whether they're my mentors or people who helped me along the way. It could just be someone I met at a bar, and that person gave me a good piece of advice, and I never meet that person again—I don't even know the person's name. I think that in small and big ways, we all can make a difference to someone else and allow them to reflect on their actions and life, and that person's going to pay it forward. So, it doesn't have to be huge, but since I'm doing this already, why not make it better?

In ARTO, we have commerce components that allow artists to optimize the IP of their works so they can repurpose their creative works into different formats like a phone cover, et cetera. And one day, since we're making things like phone covers and woven bags, I just thought—*Wait. I'm actually interested in a sustainable earth, and I don't want to create more trash. What can I do?* So, one thing we started doing is contacting this single-mum organization in India that empowers women to be self-sufficient by selling the woven bags created by them. It would be 1/10th the price if I were to buy from Alibaba and then do the same thing, and I don't have to deal with logistics. But I'm thinking, since I'm already doing this, is it possible for me to add another layer of value? Things like phone covers—can we make it with biodegradable material, or eco-friendly ink? I totally don't have to do this because it's not even my business model. In fact, it will take away more profit from us, and investors are going to complain and hate us. But the fact is, if I'm going to say that we want to create a sustainable ecosystem, bring attention to conversations that matter, and not only enable and help artists but also use art to make the world a better place, how is creating more trash making the world a better place? So to stay true to your words, you must practice it in your actions. And I think even though it will make my headway a little bit harder than the rest of the people who are just in it for the profit, we will have a more sustainable runway because we're building connections with the world around us, people who see the same vision, and people who are not just in it for the money, but believe in the world that we also believe in.

Will we build the next unicorn? Probably not. Will we have a business that's worth a few hundred million dollars at some point? Maybe yes, because it's not just about us. We're bringing in different people to build this universe we envision. Will we be successful? I don't know yet, but I'm just making my life a little bit harder this way by trying to add on layers like that. However, nothing's going to stop me.

[laughter]

MK

I like what you just shared. But I'm wondering, how does that tie in with a person's mental well-being and mental health?

Belinda

I don't know, honestly. I always think that it's overly hyped to keep telling people to be positive. I used to be one of those people, and then I realized that's the worst thing you can say to someone because you're not teaching them to accept themselves and their emotions.

MK

Yep.

Belinda

What I mean is . . . If every day you lead a positive life—you may not necessarily always have positive emotions—but you know you're doing something good and you are moving towards the direction you believe in, I think naturally, your mental health would be better.

I think people with declining mental health or with mental health struggles are living a life that isn't meant for them. Or they are not living a life that they believe in. I mean, obviously, there are people who don't have a choice, and hopefully the community can be a support system. But there are also people who are well-to-do, who may not look like they suffered any hardship in their lives, but are suffering from a lot of mental health issues. And that group is getting younger and younger. When people don't listen to one another and themselves most importantly, that's when the mind starts getting sick.

Let me give you an example. When did I find out that I wasn't very comfortable with where I was heading? When I was in between ARTO, there was a lot of talk about venture capital money and stuff like that—we still need to raise money by the way—but the entire talk was about profits and how to become the next unicorn. How to get people to take out their cheque books and write you cheques. I was not happy. Firstly, because no one was writing me a cheque yet, but mostly it was because of the people I was dealing with. They were not seeing the same world that I saw. And I didn't think they would be interested in building the company that I was interested in building. And it became a lot of marketing fluff, even from people who said 'I believe in creating a sustainable ecosystem for artists'. They were just pitching a story that they didn't mean. All they wanted in the end was profit while taking advantage of artists, and that really pissed me off. I knew that something wasn't right, that I was not happy and very uncomfortable with it. I couldn't even articulate properly because I wasn't comfortable with the idea of even articulating it.

It wasn't until I got back to my initial vision and focused on the basics, on why I started doing this in the place, what my inherent beliefs were, what my inherent value system was, that

I was able to realign with what mattered to me. Then I stopped hitting myself over things like *hey, we're moving too slowly.*

The thing with startups that fail fast is that they learn fast. They have a format that is a little bit different in the art world. In art, slow itself is an art. The process is an art. And if you fail to appreciate the slowness sometimes, then you're not necessarily appreciating art. So I began to forgive myself a little bit more even when we're slow because I know that certain things can't be rushed, and I know that there's a time for everything. So, am I worried when I don't have income? I am worried, but I am less worried and stressed than if I wasn't following my beliefs or my values or my mission in life.

YOU DON'T ASK A MACHINE HOW IT'S FEELING

MK

Let's zoom into that. How do you think that the work culture and environment in Singapore can improve in terms of mental wellness and mental health?

Belinda

I don't know whether the problem really lies in work culture. I think the problem really lies in education at home.

MK

Tell me more.

Belinda

I think the thing that forms work cultures are people. And since all of us go through the same system, that's how we are conditioned to have certain beliefs of how things should or should not work, right? And the way the entire education system was designed previously (now they're trying to change that, but it'll take another two generations) is to teach people to perform functions. In the time before AI and robots came about, humans were basically robots. There were a lot of things we learned from industrialization in Japan, and how to move towards industrialization in a short span of time. A lot of that was replicated—the way the system worked, the way they trained human beings. It was like putting humans into different assembly lines.

It's very different from today. We used to have more specialists than generalists. The pros of having specialists is that they do a job very well, but they fail to see connecting dots, and that forms a lot of misunderstandings in organisations. But at that time, families and education in our formative years were structured in such a way that people were never ever asked *how do you feel?* You don't ask your machine how it feels, right? You don't talk to your laptop that way. People were not asked about their feelings. They were judged for being right or wrong—it was black or white. And people were not rewarded for failures—only rewarded for not making mistakes. That formed a fear of judgement, making mistakes, which formed a huge imposter syndrome of being inadequate.

In Asia, there's the hierarchy of academics, jobs, and kids. It's the overall condition of society. But on the flip side, I don't think the very Americanized way is faultless too. I think they overly hype emotions, and people use that as a right. I don't necessarily think that's good, and it doesn't quite fit into our Asian culture, because we are nation before community, community before self. But in YOLO[10] countries like the US and Europe, it is me before community, community before nation. So I think that format will not work very well in our society.

But coming back to us and how I think we could potentially change . . . The education system is trying to do that right now, but because the teachers and assistants were brought up in the same era as us, they might find it difficult teaching in this new

---

[10] YOLO: You only live once

paradigm, but the inclusion of creative development, empathy development, and the way the examination system is re-designed will add value to how we approach mental health.

For work, obviously when you have more open-minded bosses and empathetic people who are in the position of employing others, policies will change, and people will be more tolerated for having flaws and vulnerability. KPIs in companies make a lot of difference. It's just like a country, right? If GDP is your one and only measurement of success, then it will always only be productivity-driven, and happiness and emotional wellbeing will not be of importance. The same thing applies in companies. If sales KPI is the only thing you measure your company against, then the entire system will be circled around that. For our overall society to have a healthy outlook, I think setting the right KPIs are very important, and it cannot be something made of just metrics.

MK

And I think that people have to change the way they look at KPI. When you talk to people, they'll say that KPI makes them stressed out. There's a lot of anxiety and fear. But KPI is just a number—how can a number make a person stressed? It is the process of reaching that KPI that brings stress. And we can look at it in two ways—one is that it's an overwhelming target that we perceive as out of our league because of our limiting beliefs. The other way is to look at it as an opportunity to overcome our limiting beliefs and create breakthroughs for ourselves by achieving things we never thought we could. And while that whole process is tough—nobody said it would be easy—it also pushes you to grow as a person.

Belinda

And also, KPI is just a word, right? Key performance indicator. But the thing is that it need not necessarily be sales. Happiness can be a KPI. Self-esteem can be a KPI. Teamwork or team happiness can be a KPI.

In my strategic communications agency, we have been working from home—it's nothing new to us. I can tell you that the productivity did not drop. We have a zero-leave policy, which means people can go on leave whenever they want, for as many days as they want, as long as the work is responsibly done and handed over, and you are doing what you need to do and performing the way you say you will perform. Actually, people go on leave less than if they had a fixed number of days off. When you have twenty-one days of leave, you feel you are obliged to finish those twenty-one, or else you're being taken advantage of by the company. But if you have zero days of leave, you know you can always go any time. You feel less inclined to escape. You don't feel that it is a need. So in my team, people don't go on MC[11]. They don't go on leave, because we're quite easy and flexible. If they need to take off, to bring their kids and parents to the hospital, it's just a phone call away. Not that they're not doing their job; just that they need to be off doing something else, and it doesn't hurt the work at all.

So, I think when people start looking at what's more important, and let's say that sales is the most important KPI, then whether or not your staff comes into work at 9 a.m. sharp in the office is not important. Why do you care if they come to work at 9 a.m. or 3 p.m., as long as they're hitting their targets? So I think sales as a KPI in terms of metrics can be good or bad. But if a company really looks at real KPIs, then a lot of the things that they're particular about don't really matter.

MENTAL HEALTH NEEDS TO COME TO A POINT WHERE WE DON'T HAVE TO TALK ABOUT IT

MK

My last question is, how can we build a more conscious ecosystem to support mental health and mental wellness?

---

[11] MC: Medical Certificate.

Belinda

I'm not sure, but I think there are some gaps or a lack of infrastructure currently, when it comes to behaviours of individuals.

I think the mental health thing is very new in Singapore. I think it was only in the last five years that people started talking about it, and COVID accelerated it. I mean, usually during economic downturns when people have problems paying bills, that's where issues happen. These issues don't happen overnight, they're just accelerated. You don't wake up the next day and suddenly have a mental health issue. That isn't what happens.

So, a few things: talking about things like this conversation we're having, helps. Most people don't talk to others about their mental issues. To be honest, all my friends know about my issues during my low points, but I haven't spoken to my family about it, because Asian families aren't actually very used to talking about serious stuff. We usually talk about what happens on TV, but we don't sit down and talk about how we feel. But I have no issues talking about this to everyone else and making this public. Even when I broke off with my boyfriend, my mum didn't know. It's just an Asian family thing. I think this kind of family dynamic has to change. I'm starting to see it in a lot of my friends with younger kids because they're new-generation parents, and they have a new form of parenting that's a lot more open with a stronger emphasis on empathy and compassion.

But for a start, there are certain things in our comfort zone we can do, even if we are not comfortable speaking with our direct family or speaking with friends. The way you express yourself— there's a difference between expressing and sharing your mental journey versus ranting and complaining. Haha! I think what we need to do is stop ranting and complaining. That spreads really bad energy, and nobody wants to be beside someone with really bad energy. I think ranting and complaining is more defensive than being vulnerable. If we are more willing to be vulnerable— it doesn't matter if it's with family, friends, or somebody you meet at a bar—and you find somebody you can trust with your expressions, and you make an effort to find your own support group, that vulnerability will bring us forward in our mental health journey.

The other thing I told you before on a personal basis, MK, is that I feel there's a huge lack of awareness of low-grade chronic mental issues. I think that there's an increased awareness in clinical mental health, clinical depression or bipolar disorder, situations that require medication, and stuff like that. But I think most people don't associate themselves with those characteristics and traits and don't think they have those issues. But at some point in time, you're going to be stressed out in life, and you don't want to go home and start lashing out at your husband and kids and just lose it because of all the stress and negativity buried inside you. So should mental health be looked at like flu seasons? If your body can get sick, so can your mind. The fundamental gap currently is to highlight the awareness of chronic mental health issues like chronic depression, stress, and anger management. People need to understand that if you are unnecessarily angry or stressed all the time, you need to seek help. Or if you can't sleep five out of seven days a week and you come home and start lashing at your kids, you need help. Or you always feel fatigued and feel very down, you need help. It doesn't mean that you need to be clinically diagnosed or on medication before you need help.

And is that help readily available? I don't think so. I think that the current system doesn't allow people to pursue a sustainable career as a therapist. If you're a psychiatrist or psychologist, you get paid a lot. But if you're a therapist or counsellor, you get paid peanuts. So, a lot of people don't want to get into that. A lot of therapists and counsellors are fresh graduates from school who haven't yet been through life enough. They don't really understand all these issues people are having. So I think some ways we can bridge this gap is to bring in foreign experts or incentivise mid-career changes and train people.

And even though therapists and counsellors are not medical professionals, they should be considered medical professionals. Like how an optometrist is technically not a doctor, but can diagnose eye issues. I think that they need to be respected as very important members of the medical ecosystem. They are your first gatekeepers before anything more serious happens. I think some of these therapists and counsellors should be made more accessible to schools without the labelling and branding. They should be like dentist in schools where it's okay to go and students are scheduled to go for ten-minute or fifteen-minute sessions, so that they develop the habit that it's okay, it's not a scary thing, and parents don't have the stigma that, 'Oh she's seeing a psychiatrist, she's seeing a doctor, she's siao[12]'. That's the problem. We need to cultivate the mindset that it's okay for my mind to catch a flu. I'm just getting treatment for my flu, and then in three months I'm going to be fine. I think when that kind of mindset is established, people will be more accepting of mental health.

Mental health needs to come to a point where we don't have to talk about it—it's just the flu. That's the best situation.

---

[12] Siao: Local slang for crazy.

CHAPTER 4

Mental Health From the Perspective of a Father

By Desmond Chew, Caregiver, Caregivers Alliance Limited

Desmond is the caregiver for his son, who suffers from anxiety issues. He shares his journey from discovering his son's illness, coming to terms with it, and then joining a support group by the Caregivers Alliance. Desmond shares candidly some of the challenges he faced as a caregiver, and would like to share with other caregivers to not give up hope on recovery for their loved ones.

CAREGIVING FOR MY SON

Si Qi

Hi Desmond! Can you tell me more about your journey as a caregiver?

Desmond

During my son's fifth year in his integrated programme, he started developing some anxiety issues. He went to see a psychiatrist, who happened to be the SAF MO[13] who attended to him later as well. He finished his A levels, went to NS, and that's when the anxiety got worse. After his first month of enlistment, he was referred to IMH and then the Military Medicine Institute at Kent Ridge. The medical leaves given to him got more frequent and longer until he seemed to be staying at home most of the time. My son shared with us his intention to request for exemption from NS as he felt it was the only solution at that time for him to recover. My wife and I also wanted our son to recover very badly, so we went ahead to sign the exemption letter. My son rested at home for less than a year and I am glad that he managed to overcome his difficulties. Right now, he's in his final year at NTU[14] studying sociology.

Si Qi

Thank you for sharing that. Were there any struggles with being a caregiver?

Desmond

In the beginning, I thought my son was just trying all means to get out of NS, and it wasn't until we got the diagnosis from the doctor that I realized that he's really not feeling well. For me, it

---

[13] SAF MO: Singapore Armed Forces Medical Officer

[14] NTU: Nanyang Technological University

didn't affect my emotions a lot. I just tried to think of ways to help him when he's having an anxiety attack. It's my wife who got very emotionally affected. She didn't even dare to share with her own sister about my son's condition. She got very worried about his future and sometimes got really depressed. *Will he be able to get a job? Will he be able to recover?* As she was looking for more information about my son's condition and caregiving support, she decided to join the C2C[15] class organized by Caregivers Alliance and persuaded me to join so that we could work together to support our son.

Si Qi

I want to understand more from you what it's like to be a caregiver, because as you know, Singapore is an ageing society. More people will find themselves in a caregiver's role, and we may not be equipped to take it on because it can happen to anyone and any time.

Desmond

I consider myself a secondary caregiver. My wife is the primary caregiver who drives him to the doctor, who takes care of the medication, and is always spending time with him. My struggle is financial, because every visit to the doctor is a few hundred dollars, with the medications and all. Although I'm able to afford it, the financial strain can be very tough on other caregivers.

As a father, it was also about getting used to being more sensitive to my son, as compared to my wife who would know if he was uncomfortable with just one look. In the beginning when we had meals outside, we had to avoid crowds and anything related to the army, like a SAFRA[16] restaurant. But me being me,

---

[15] C2C: Caregivers-to-Caregivers

[16] SAFRA: Social and recreational facilities and clubs for National Servicemen

I'm not that sensitive to all that. If we promised to bring him to a less crowded place and we see an unexpected crowd when we reach, he will feel that *wah we've broken a promise*, but I wouldn't notice all that happening. I did feel a bit *pek cek*[17] that I had to get used to a different lifestyle. His mother does a better job at that. She will kick me when we're eating to tell me that my son isn't feeling well. Otherwise, I would still be eating.

In the beginning, you will feel like *aiyah, why must you do this?* But I must admit that I'm very lucky because in these one or two years, we didn't face many problems except that we needed to avoid crowds. Once, I brought him out to cycle. It totally slipped my mind that we had to cross a very busy traffic junction. When we reached the junction, he suddenly sped off away from me. I simply could not catch up with him and I lost him. He came back home later and said that he couldn't stand the crowds. But so far I'm lucky. We didn't experience any behavioural problems and violence like what other caregivers might have to go through.

Si Qi

Actually, a lot of parents might find it hard to accept if their child is having a mental health issue. Even going to IMH to see a psychologist is hard to accept for many people. How did you come to learn and accept your son?

Desmond

For me, it was okay. It was much harder for my wife to accept his condition—a lot of thoughts went through her mind. When he took a long MC away from NS, she was initially hoping that he could at least complete half of his NS training so he can get the National Service certificate. Unfortunately, he had to be

---

[17] Pek cek: Singapore slang for irritated, exasperated, frustrated

exempted from NS before getting his certificate. So my wife even wondered if future employers would know that he didn't do NS and ask him about it.

For me, I didn't feel the same way. I was willing to share with my friends and family about it. Being in a big family with many cousins, I told them in advance to avoid the topic of NS when they came over for Chinese New Year.

Si Qi

And that communication is really important, right? Because that way you get to enjoy Chinese New Year as per usual. And it's nice that everyone was so understanding of the situation.

Desmond

It was not so much to enjoy. I was more worried that the situation would be awkward for my family.

Si Qi

I'm so moved by what you did. You really held everyone together. Your family, your wife, and your son.

Desmond

Alright lah, I mean that's what I can do, because she is the main person looking after him, I only pay for the medical fees. I cannot walk out of my work life to look after him. The only thing I can do is to support my wife, that's all. If I look after my wife, then my wife can look after our son.

IT FELT LIKE A DEATH SENTENCE TO US

Si Qi

Yeah, everyone plays their part. Okay, so going back to the C2C programme, what did you guys learn, what were the activities in the programme?

Desmond

I missed out one point just now. When we first saw the doctor, and I think this is something that affects many caregivers, the doctor said 'No, there is no cure for this illness'. This is very—

Si Qi

Like a stab in the heart.

Desmond

The doctor probably didn't mean that there's no recovery, but to any caregiver or any parent, it really feels like a death sentence to us.

My son knows his medication. He knows the side effects. He knows he has to tell his doctor what's happening to him. And once he showed the medicine to my parents and jokingly told them 这个是那个神经病的人吃的 (this is what people who are mentally ill eat). But my parents, being old folks, immediately told me that 'Desmond, you better don't let him eat this medicine, he's going to eat for life', which is one of the common misconceptions about medication for mental illness. Before we knew our child had this condition, our knowledge was very limited.

What the C2C programme teaches us is that recovery is possible for a lot of mental health illnesses. It gives us a light at the end of the tunnel, although the level of recovery varies. To someone, the patient taking his medication on time every day is a certain level of recovery already. Some people might want their loved ones to recover to how they were like in the past. For my son, he's finishing his degree, and he has been taking his medication until last year when he consulted his doctor to try to stop the medication. Everybody's recovery is different.

Another important thing C2C teaches is empathy. We learn that sometimes how he thinks, what he says and how he behaves is not up to him. It's the imbalance of his brain's chemicals that tells him or makes him do certain things. The programme teaches us to separate the illness from our loved ones. That's what also motivated me to become a volunteer with Caregivers Alliance. Because we have many caregivers telling us 'Desmond, the lessons on listening and communicating really work. My son is much calmer after I listen to him patiently, and I know my son now'. It's very heartwarming to hear all this.

NEVER GIVE UP HOPE ON OUR LOVED ONES

Si Qi

Anything else you would like to share about your story?

Desmond

I keep saying that I'm very lucky because when I joined CAL[18], I saw so many people suffering in this situation. A lot of people still have stigma towards mental health illnesses. So right now, whenever I go out with my friends, I'll always tell them that I'm volunteering with CAL and that my son was once not feeling well. It's okay to share actually. We must overcome our own stigma when dealing with our loved ones so that other people won't make it worse. As long as we face it upfront, we will always overcome the illness.

Si Qi

Nice. If you had one message you would like to share with people about mental health, what would that be?

Desmond

Don't give up hope on our loved ones. There is always help, and there is a chance they can recover with proper medication and care.

For caregivers, do take care of yourselves. We need to take care of ourselves to take care of them. Self-care is not selfish.

---

[18] CAL: Caregivers Alliance Limited

Many caregivers feel guilty about doing self-care. They would feel that they can't enjoy themselves when their loved one is suffering. But we can. So self-care is important. Keep ourselves healthy!

Si Qi

Thank you so much for your time, I enjoyed speaking with you.

CHAPTER 5

Coming to Terms with Caregiving

By Jacqueline, Caregiver

Jacqueline noticed that her mother was showing signs of dementia when she began staying at home after quitting her job in 2013. But it took her a few years before she finally accepted that her mother was suffering from mental deterioration, and that she had to become a caregiver. Her mother was diagnosed in 2019 January, and her brother passed away in 2019 July. She suddenly found herself to be the sole caregiver for her mother, and had to face the challenges of that role on her own. She grew to accept her mother for who she is, instead of trying to change her. And with this newfound sense of patience and acceptance, she was able to spend a peaceful Circuit Breaker together with her mother.

COMING TO TERMS WITH CAREGIVING

MK

Alright, so first question. Tell me about your journey as a caregiver.

Jacqueline

So initially, I wasn't consciously aware that I had become a caregiver. In 2013 when I quit my job, I was staying home first and that was when I realized that my mum's memory was actually so bad. She couldn't remember how to take the bus to visit friends or go to Mustafa or City Hall, places that she used to go. It's just a straight bus or straight train from our place to City Hall or Mustafa and she forgot which stop to get off at. Got off at the wrong stop and walked for hours, but she kept thinking that it's just a little bit further ahead, things like that. So at that time, I didn't think of myself as a caregiver. But then I realized that *oh maybe it's a good thing that I quit my job. I can like help my mum a bit more.* I think I had the typical kind of caregiver anxiety. I wasn't aware of it, but it was this over-worrying about what's happening to her, trying to think of things to do with her, or asking her to do things to prevent her from losing her memory and slowing down her memory loss or whatever lah, you know. And I didn't recognize it then, but my *kanchiong*-ness[19] was actually making my mother's condition worse. So to cut the long story short, I saw a movie about Alzheimer's. I also read a book that somebody had passed to me, and coincidentally the themes were about elderly people going through old age, dementia, memory loss and all that, and I began to recognize some of the signs in my mum.

In 2014 when I was on a retreat, many of these pieces of the puzzle seemed to fall into place for me and I realized that I just have to decide now, I have to accept now, the worst possible thing

---

[19] Kanchiong: Singapore slang for paranoia

that could happen to my mum. I realized that actually, no matter what happens, I still want to look after her. And that realization made me feel much better. And I no longer had that kanchiongness about her condition. I just thought, whatever happens to her, I will look after her. I also recognized that actually, she's probably partially aware of her condition and concerned about it too, and my being kanchiong about it was making her feel worse. So when I got home from the retreat, I had a change of mindset about it and I stopped giving my mum a hard time about whether she's doing things to improve her memory. I just let her be and I became okay with however she is because I thought well, whatever it is, I will look after her. And then I noticed a dramatic shift. She seemed to become so much better. She seemed to forget less, which sort of reinforced my understanding that when they're stressed, it actually exacerbates their symptoms of memory loss because I'm just creating more confusion in her mind.

A couple of years later, I started to attend different courses whenever I could. I attended a course where there was a sharing by caregivers about persons with disabilities. There were two case studies written in first person. One was written in first person of the person with Alzheimer's, and the other was written in first person of the caregiver. And the two stories hit home so hard, I couldn't stop crying in that course because I was really . . . [voice cracking, Jacqueline begins to cry] *Oh man.* I think at that time, I sort of finally really accepted that my mum has some sort of mental health condition, like some mental deterioration that became very stark but she still hadn't been diagnosed yet. And you know when people have Alzheimer's, dementia and all, they get very stubborn. They get very one-track minded. If they want to do something, they will keep doing it, but if they don't want to do something, they just won't do at all. She didn't want to see a doctor, so I couldn't persuade her to see a doctor. And in talking about it to friends and all that, one friend of mine said that she's gone for this course with CAL[20]. It's a very comprehensive 12-week programme. I started going, and with time, I realized it was the best thing I ever did. By the second week, my mother was like, 'Oh, where are you going? I'll come with you'. So my mother would come and sit in on the course with me. [laughing] It was very cute. They even gave her a certificate of attendance. And they still support my mum, and she still comes to all the courses. I didn't recognize back then how big it was. Because it's not like you learn something in the course and it just changes your mind overnight. I felt the lessons were kind of seeping in over a year. When we learn something, I would be like, *oh, I see the effect of what they said.* There were lessons on communication. One of them was reflective responses, and I never understood reflective responses. The way it's taught, it almost sounds like I'm supposed to reflect back to the person what they said. So initially, all I got was, am I supposed to just repeat what they said back at them? So they say 'Oh you know, I had a bad time, this person yelled at me'. So I say 'Oh, you had a bad time? This person yelled at you?' That's what I thought reflective responses were, but it seemed very weird. But over the years, I realized that it's not just about parroting back what they say, it's about recognising the emotions that's hidden in their words that they can't express.

So my journey began as a caregiver in January 2019 when my mother said she had a lot of pain all over her body and she wanted to see a doctor. So we went to see a doctor at the polyclinic and then my mum was rambling so much and she said 'I have very bad headaches' and all that. So then the doctor pounced on that and he arranged for her to go to the neuro and they confirmed that she had Alzheimer's, that she had massive brain deterioration. So my mum's brain was apparently like just a little more than half gone. The doctor was even surprised that she was still fully

---

[20] CAL: Caregivers Alliance Limited

functional, and he said just her initial brain reserves must have been huge. So my mum recognises she has dementia, that she has some Alzheimer's. And she's kind of special because you know, with the amount of brain space she has left, she's still doing good whereas another person might be catatonic. And she's very accepting of it, so that's very helpful, and she takes responsibility. She walks like 10k steps every day at least, 10–20k. And like what I said about people with dementia, when they set their sights on something, they *die die*[21] also will do. If they don't want to do, they die die won't do. So she die die also will walk. I think I'm blessed that way that she's very active and it helps with her condition. If it gets too gloomy in the house, she'll be like 'Let's go walking and then we'll all feel better'. That's her thing.

WHERE IS THE LOVE?

Jacqueline

So after my mum was diagnosed in January 2019, my brother died in July 2019. And I think that's when I became a full-time caregiver because suddenly, there was just me. I had a lot of frustration trying to cope with my mum.

I think something that caregivers go through is that you get really frustrated by the lack of logic when you're talking to your loved ones, and you still try to persuade them or get them to try and see reason. Sometimes they have a meltdown because they've had it with what they perceive to be opposing views. But I think in part, it's us not accepting that our loved one is not capable of logic anymore. We still hope that they are, because we don't want them to have bad thoughts or whatever it is, you know what I mean? And I would say for about six months after my brother passed away, my mother was in a very bad state. Her paranoia was

---

[21] Die die: Singapore slang that implies a person will definitely do something, by hook or by crook

out of the world. And to the point, to this day, my husband can't come to my mum's house anymore and all that because [voice begins to crack] she thinks he's taken things from her house, or stealing her money, and stuff like that. And I recognize that you know, a doctor told me that she's kind of suffering from both dementia and depression from my brother's death and the shock of all that. So I realize that actually, it's insecurity. She's worried that I, the sole living relative of hers, would be taken away also, so she needs to find a reason that I shouldn't be taken away. So my husband becomes the person who might take me away, and she needs to make him into a bad person. Luckily, my husband is very supportive and understanding, so he didn't take it personally or badly. He understood right away the situation and we've managed to keep it at an even keel. But yeah, in those six months, I had a hard time coping and sometimes felt really down but my support system, my friends, my husband, my mum-in-law, they're really great. And I have a friend who's a psychiatrist who's also teaching me to do things like gratitude exercises every morning and night when things are bad. I was doing it because I was in such a bad mental state, I just needed things to help me and I think some glimmer of positivity comes back into the mind over time.

And during the Circuit Breaker, I couldn't see my husband for eight weeks. But I don't know what to put it down to, whether it's the grace of all the gratitude practice I did, or the grace of the universe, or desperation is the mother of invention, or whatever. The evening before the Circuit Breaker kicked in, she was saying her usual things about feeling like she should kill herself and people would be happier if she's dead, she doesn't want to be a burden and all that. And usually, I would get very distressed when she says all these things. I would always feel like whatever I do is not enough, that's why she says these things. But that day, I don't know, I sat there and looked at her and looked in my mind and thought, *where is the love, you know? Where?* I needed to speak to her from some place of love that she is not experiencing, because my distress clearly is just anger, right? So then I looked at her and realized that oh, she's distressed. My mum needs reassurance. She feels like she's not worthy of love, or being looked after. And somehow when I saw that she was in distress, rather than *I'm not good enough*, then finally the right words came to me and I was able to reassure her *that I want to be there for her, I want to look after her*, you know, *she's not a burden*. I reminded her of how she looked after us when we were younger, what a good mother she's been to us, and all that. She rehashed some old stories about things that she perceived as other people setting up barriers between us and all that. And again, I was able to not react to the story and just let her speak, just let her be. And that calmed her down. So we spent a very peaceful Circuit Breaker together.

After that, it's just continued sort of that way. I recognized more and more the emotions from which mum spoke, rather than see her words as a judgement against me. I started volunteering with CAL, co-facilitating the 12-week course for caregivers with persons of mental health illnesses and I find that very rewarding because just interacting with the class, interacting with the trainer from CAL, I learn so many lessons and I also feel supported by the network of people I'm with.

MK

Nice. Jacqueline, one question I would like to ask you is this: how do you think caregivers, even yourself, can better take care of their emotional and mental needs?

Jacqueline

I think having the right people to talk to about it and the right feedback about it is very important. And sometimes cognitive input isn't enough. I found that my anxiety levels were getting so high, I was having this kind of low-level persistent negative thinking that I couldn't shake, and it was really getting me down. I would wake up with this feeling of dread very often. It was getting to the point where I was scared the feeling would come and that itself was another thing. I felt I was derailing, like I was losing my mind. Facilitating the caregivers' classes, you learn about all the mental health illnesses. It just felt like I might be on the brink of one, you know. My best friend set up an appointment for me with a naturopath, and it's actually just been four weeks now but it's since helped a lot. So I say to caregivers, be really sensitive to the state of your mental health. If just talking to friends or being with family, or whatever you do generally helps, great. But sometimes if you need other kinds of help, seek help. There's no stigma to it. Because it's only when we're in a good frame of mind that we can help our loved ones properly. I can tell that on days when I'm in a good frame of mind, my mother is in a better frame of mind too because she's just bouncing emotions off me.

DO YOU SEE THE PERSON OR THE CONDITION?

MK

Your sharing was really, really powerful. I'm very moved by it. I think you are also standing in the position of a trainer, correct? Sometimes you train the other caregivers as well?

Jacqueline

Yeah.

MK

What are some things that you observe that caregivers often miss out as a blind spot?

Jacqueline

I would say for the caregivers who are not coping well, what they often miss out is that their own emotions are getting in the way of understanding their loved ones better. When we understand our loved ones better, it sets up a more harmonious kind of relationship because we can relate to them from a different point of view. We start to see them as people, not just someone who's disabled but someone who also has feelings. They also don't want to be a burden. They want to be helpful, and sometimes some of the annoying things they seem to be doing might be things that they're trying to do to help us, you know. They want to contribute, they're just not very effective at it. So it's usually our emotions that get in the way.

But I also find that almost in every class I've gone to, more than half the class will be filled with caregivers who are coping well, and in each case they've all been very observant. They have noticed the changes in their loved ones, and they have also interpreted what they noticed in their loved ones correctly, which means they understand their loved ones and what's happening. And the process of understanding our loved ones comes in bits and pieces. It's not like suddenly you understand everything—it comes slowly. I think it boils down to them not getting emotional or too hung up. They have no stigma towards their loved ones' conditions. The first trainer, when I went for the first C2C, talked a lot about how he told his neighbours about his son's condition. He told his friends, and he said 'You'll be surprised that everyone has someone that they know or that they're caring for who has a mental condition', and they understand. They won't stigmatize you. In fact, they become a source of support and help. I think that's a big one. I tell my mum's friends so that they are better able to understand how to positively interact with her. I don't try to control their interactions, but I tell them what her condition is and how she interprets things so that they can see that *oh okay, she's not just being weird or rude*. It takes the burden off. It helps people see that you're not just sick, you're also a person who has a sense of pride and shame.

MK

Got it, got it. Thank you, Jacqueline. Now, the final question would be this. If you had a message to the public, to the world, whether it is to caregivers or people who have family members suffering from Alzheimer's, what would you tell them?

Jacqueline

Wow, that's a deep one. [laughing] I don't know actually, what would I say to me? I think. What would I say to me that would be helpful?

[silence, Jacqueline pondering]

Jacqueline

I guess I'd say you're not alone. Yeah. And if you need help, please seek help. It's the best thing you can do for yourself and your loved ones.

CHAPTER 6

Weaving A Tapestry of Support

By Nicole K, Founder, The Tapestry Project

Nicole was diagnosed with depression and anxiety in 2006, and back then she couldn't find many personal stories of people with mental health conditions in Singapore. That inspired her to start the Tapestry Project to collect personal stories, advice and perspectives from people with mental health conditions. She founded the project in 2014, and continues to run the online publication till today as her way of paying it forward for the support she has received in her own recovery journey.

STORIES BEHIND THE STATISTICS

MK

I'm interested in why you do what you do. How has your experience running the mental health publication been so far?

Nicole

The Tapestry Project officially started in 2014, but the journey began much earlier. I was diagnosed with depression and anxiety in 2006, and back then, I didn't have a very good first experience with the psychiatrist. At that time, personal stories were very limited. Nobody was talking about mental health from a lived experience point of view, and if you googled, you only got information and personal stories from the States. But what I needed at that time was someone who could tell me who to go to for help in Singapore, or how to save money to afford treatment. This knowledge was not so accessible back then.

More importantly, I didn't know that I could switch psychiatrists. So for a lot of people who are seeking professional help, they might assume that the first doctor they see is going to 'cure' them. But mental health is a bit more complex because it's more than just a medical issue. It is related to your environment, your social systems, and the psychosocial aspects of it. So having good chemistry and rapport with your doctor or psychologist is very important.

My first experience was quite bad because the psychiatrist didn't even make eye contact with me. She took notes, asked me to fill up a form, and she concluded that I had mild depression even though I told her that I wanted to die. If that's not suicidal intent or ideation, then I don't know what is. I think one of the issues was that I was young. I was only twenty-three or twenty-four, and perhaps at that point in time, practitioners were not so enlightened to the fact that youths did suffer from such things.

There could be 101 reasons behind why she responded that way to me. Then me, being an uninformed patient, I just unassumingly listened to her. I took one week of Prozac and came back the following week as she asked. I entered a room where there were ten–twelve interns sitting in an auditorium just observing me and writing down notes as she spoke to me. I felt so humiliated. I felt that Nicole didn't exist anymore—she's just reduced to a diagnosis, a stack of case notes, and a statistic.

Because of this experience, I decided to start the Tapestry Project. I felt that part of what contributes to stigma comes from people not being able to relate to the information presented to them. We see all these statistics like, one in ten, one in eight, but what does it really mean? How does it relate to a person when they themselves need help? That's why I feel that while statistics are important in informing certain decisions, they don't really offer an accurate understanding of mental health and they don't represent the nuanced needs that a person might require help with. That's why I thought we needed to talk about the stories behind each statistic and I wanted to make it as accessible to anyone as possible, which is why the Tapestry Project is in a digital format, so that anyone with an internet connection will be able to access these stories.

MENTAL HEALTH IS A SPECTRUM

MK

I want to ask you something from the angle of peer support. What do people misunderstand the most about supporting people through their mental health struggles?

Nicole

I think there's a lot of pressure to 'fix' that struggling person. But mental health is a spectrum. It's not something you either have or don't have, or something you recover from or don't, or something that determines if you're 'weak' or 'strong'. I find that these dichotomous mindsets are the ones that can be quite harmful when it comes to mental health and stigma. Nobody wants to fall in either camp, right? But if we could all change our mindsets to see that mental health is a spectrum, a dynamic concept, it means that there are seasons when you need to receive help, and seasons when you can give help.

In relation to what you asked about peer support, as friends, they might feel pressured to help 'fix' that person. This mindset leads to firstly feeling inadequate, feeling like *oh no, I can't handle this because I'm not trained.* Or secondly, feeling burnt out from making sure that this person becomes 100 per cent 'okay'. I say this from personal experience, as someone who has supported other people before I myself was diagnosed. I don't know whether it's some sort of complex, but it naturally happens because you care a lot about the person and you just want to do your best for them. But I think whoever is playing that supportive role should also know that you're just there to support, and not to fix them.

LEANING INTO DISCOMFORT

MK

You literally just answered my next question. I wanted to ask you about what would be a more constructive way of supporting people who are struggling with their mental health. A lot of times, in the environment we live in, people are too quick to make conclusions, judgements, and give answers even if the answers don't address the root cause of the issue. Maybe what the other person needs is the space for them to express themselves and for somebody to just listen and be there for them. But oftentimes when we are too quick to make judgements and conclusions, we are no longer there with that person. There's a disengagement, a disconnect. I think it's bad because we stop connecting with the other person. What do you think?

Nicole

I totally get what you mean. When you share something, people are not really there to listen because they want to listen, but because they already have something in mind and they just want to say what they want to say instead of holding space for you. I think people are just not comfortable with leaning into their discomfort and in dealing with uncertainty.

I wonder if there's something lacking in the way we are educating ourselves when it comes to mental health. We do have the head knowledge. We know it's a medical issue. But it also has the more complex and nuanced psychosocial elements. We ask people to seek help and speak out, but we're not really trained to listen.

So back to addressing stigma. Part of it is education, and the other part is empowering the other person to be able to lean in and truly listen. But to be frank, some people just aren't comfortable talking about feelings and mental health, and I don't think we should force it on them.

MK

That's why listening is a skill, to be able to hear it for what it is without any personal filters.

Nicole

And be unafraid to say that you don't understand. To help people, you can't go in there saying, 'I know everything; here's my solution'. It's like what you say—it creates a disconnect the moment people do that.

CATCHING THE EARLY SIGNS

MK

Interesting. There's a huge divide and a misconception around what mental health is and what mental health is not. From running the publication and receiving stories from people on the ground, from all walks of life, what are the misconceptions people have about mental health?

Nicole

That's a bit complex. A lot to unpack.

MK

You can start from wherever you wish.

Nicole

I think it has evolved over the years. I have been doing this for about six years, coming to seven. I don't feel that it's that long, but it is. Maybe it's passion, I don't know. It just doesn't feel like it's work.

I remember the first story I received. This person wrote about her childhood, and I remember being very touched by it. It doesn't explicitly talk about mental illness. So that's what Tapestry is trying to do. We don't want to put labels on things and say things like, 'oh I have schizophrenia and I hear voices'. We want to avoid that sort of narrative. So what she wrote was very heartfelt, and I feel it is a good sign that people are starting to grasp that concept. We didn't get that many stories last time, and I had to beg my friends and ask 'Can you please submit your story?'

I also felt a bit depressed that I had so many friends who were depressed that I could ask for stories, like 'eh, why you all got issues?' [laughing] I don't think it's because I attract depressed people, but rather, it is the power of vulnerability and being authentic. When you share your own struggles, it gives people the permission to share their struggles as well, so that's why my friends talk to me about their own issues. We definitely have more stories now, but it's still not enough. We're trying to publish one every week, but it's very difficult because everybody is doing the same thing now and only the same pool of people is sharing.

But going back to your question. One of the misconceptions about mental health is that it is an all-or-nothing concept, that you either have mental health or you don't, that you either recover or you don't. But mental health is a work in progress. A spectrum, and a dynamic thing. We're all works in progress, whether we have mental illnesses or not.

MK

What are also some of the ugly truths about yourself that you had to face in order to move forward in your battle against depression?

Nicole

It's the constant 'imposter syndrome'. I constantly feel that I'm not doing things fast enough, not smart enough, not good enough, so I can be quite punishing to myself. But I think over the years, with many years of therapy, lots of self-help books and a lot of prayer and support, I find that I am kinder to myself now and I've learnt to not take myself so seriously. There's a difference between taking your work seriously and taking yourself seriously.

MK

Some people might think that their mental health struggles are just small issues that they can deal with by themselves, and unfortunately it can sometimes become a big issue. And it is only when things get worse do people start seeking help. From your personal experience, what do you think are the consequences of not seeking help early?

Nicole

I'll share about my dog. I had a spaniel, Chloe, and I've had her for seven to eight years already, so she's a senior dog.

She had really bad skin infections, and I thought, *I'll just bring her to the vet and get her some medicated shampoo.* In the end, after many years of treatment, she still had all these recurring infections.

She was losing a lot of weight and energy. I asked the vet about what was going on, and the vet said that it could be food allergies since her ear and skin infections kept recurring. That's when I learnt that animals could be allergic to food, which I didn't know about. If I had known earlier, I would have stopped feeding her certain things, and her infections wouldn't have gotten so bad.

So I think it's similar to mental health—when you don't catch the early signs of emotional distress, when you keep doing the same thing, approaching things the same way, you start to sweep things under the carpet, or you rationalize that things are not a big issue when they actually are. This sets us up for a disaster because you're not addressing the underlying issue, and very soon, the things you sweep under your carpet will become this giant mountain of pus, like an infection that you have to deal with. So when I look back and reflect, I should have persisted in seeking help, instead of giving up on the first get go.

After I saw that first psychiatrist, I was still thinking that *it's no big deal,* that I just had to suck it up and deal with it. Yet I couldn't, because I kept thinking that *I'm such a failure, I'm such a disappointment.* At the same time, I was also berating myself into thinking positive and being grateful. Because of all these internal narratives and stories I was telling myself, I only got proper help in 2011. That's a good number of years lost. If I had persisted in seeking help over deceivingly little things and the smaller symptoms, I think I would have had fewer losses in life. But I'm still grateful it all happened the way it did.

That's my long-winded way of addressing your question. Get help early before it festers. Treatment is there, help is readily available. Sometimes you've just got to keep trying to find that right fit. I know it can be very tiring and quite disheartening sometimes when you feel that professional help, your friends, or family are not available to you. But I believe one should persist and fight for one's own recovery.

MK

In your understanding of what mental health is in relation to a person's overall wellbeing, where do treatments such as counselling and therapy fit in?

Nicole

I think therapy is for everyone. I think the world would be a much better place if we had therapy for everyone. [laughing] Everybody has baggage. There are things in life that will disappoint you and we carry these wounds with us. When we don't address these wounds, they fester. So therapy would help take off some of the burden, and the best thing about therapists is that they are trained to help you navigate, dissect, and heal from these wounds. We can talk to our family and friends, but they may not necessarily be able to provide that extra layer of help that we need.

Medication wise, when we talk about mental health professionals, there's the psychiatrist who gives medication, and then there's the therapy aspect which includes your psychologists, psychotherapists, and counsellors. I think personally, I would turn to therapy first. If that doesn't work, then I would also consult a psychiatrist to see if medication can solve some of these issues.

MK

You were saying that you would turn to therapy first instead of psychiatry. Why is that?

Nicole

There are limitations when it comes to accessibility and relief. Medication has side effects, and it's expensive. Plus, it takes a certain period before the full benefits of the medication kick in. So I imagine that going for therapy would be a much easier first step for people when it comes to help-seeking, and if that isn't sufficient, then medication is the next step as a treatment option.

MK

What else do you think a person should do to maintain their mental health?

Nicole

Are you familiar with the diathesis stress model?

MK

Tell me more about it.

Nicole

So the assumption is, you are born with certain genetics—that there's a genetic element when it comes to mental illnesses. There's the biological and the biographical. The biological aspect refers to your genetic inheritance; the biographical aspect refers to your life's events. So, the diathesis stress model assumes that people with a genetic predisposition are more likely to be triggered by adverse life events and experience mental ill health.

A person can be totally 'mentally healthy', so to speak, and yet still be overcome by life circumstances such as the passing of someone you love, or a retrenchment. It could even be a 'happy' event, like getting a job promotion or having a baby. It doesn't mean that your mental health is 'weak'—it just means that the stress is overwhelming your existing resources. That's something I think people can reflect on.

In terms of maintaining myself—maintaining my own sanity—I try to make time to do frivolous things like gardening, petting my cat, going for walks, and laughing a lot. I also make sure I take my medication every day. I check in with my therapist quite regularly. I journal a lot too, so that I don't keep things in. Whenever I feel very frustrated about something or I can't seem to wrap my head around certain issues, I'll journal to externalize everything.

PAYING IT FORWARD

MK

Nicole, is there anything else you wish to add to this interview?

Nicole

I want to know your story.

MK

I began searching for answers after experiencing a quarter-life crisis when I was eighteen. I realized that money can only bring you so far, and that there are other aspects of life that we have been neglecting for too long. That's why I've been channeling a lot of my energy into different social causes. It is my way to pay forward my experiences so that people have the clarity to walk the path they are meant to walk.

After completing National Service, I went on to study engineering in university. But after my first year, I dropped out because I realized that engineering was what my teachers and my parents expected me to do, just because I was good in mathematics and physics. But it wasn't truly what I wanted for myself. I left and went to do architecture because I wanted to find out if it was possible to combine and integrate physical spaces with higher consciousness as an experience, such that anybody present in the space can be connected deeply within themselves, with their deepest truths—even if it was for just one moment in their lives. I had a hypothesis and I went into architecture to verify that, and I travelled to Japan, China and Switzerland to train under a few architects. Long story short, when I was in Japan, I verified that my hypothesis could be achieved.

I came back and worked in the corporate architecture field. The work hours in Singapore were crazy. We were working from 8.30 a.m. to 4.30 a.m. every day, and we were expected to come back at 8.30 a.m. the next day. I mean, you leave your office at 4.30 a.m. By the time you take a cab home and shower, it's already about 5.45 a.m. If you come into the office at 8.45 a.m., your boss will ask why you're late. In the design world, it's normal. Because it's normal, you're expected to do so. But I couldn't reconcile that. I loved designing, I loved architecture, but did I want to sit behind this giant Mac computer working for somebody else's dreams, when deep down inside me, all I wanted to do was make a difference to people? The whole point of wanting to combine physical spaces with higher consciousness was to create a zen space for people to truly reconnect to themselves. There are so many zombies out there, especially on the train. Look into their eyes. The eyes are the windows to a person's soul. How many of them are still alive?

Nicole

It's like the lights are on, but nobody's home.

MK

Exactly. Nobody's home. And what a pity. If we're not really here, in this moment, then where are we? If we can't even be here with another person, with our lovers, with our parents, it means we are stuck in the past. Physically, we are here. But mentally and emotionally, our soul isn't here. How does that work? Doesn't it also affect our relationships with ourselves?

That was when I realized that I really had to do my work. I couldn't continue to be small when I knew I had bigger dreams of wanting to make a difference to people. I asked myself, *if today were to be the last day of my life, can I say that I have lived a worthwhile life?* I realized that if I didn't live true to who I was, I wouldn't be able to say so. All I wanted to do was to live a life I could say I really lived. It was always about making a difference to people, so I spent my time and energy training myself in transformational work and life coaching.

As I was chasing after my own healing and transformation, I found certain truths and I just thought, *what would be different if the world could see what I saw?* And the only reason I could see the things I saw was because I had great teachers who were guiding me. It didn't come from me alone. So I knew that in a way, that was a gift that somebody passed on to me. A gift is meant to be given away, so I wanted to pass it on.

If the work that we do can stop a person from committing suicide, even just one person, then I think we have done our part. One life saved can save many others. That's what I'm really after.

Nicole

How do you maintain your own mental wellness? I imagine there's a lot of emotional labour in the work that you do?

MK

It's got to do with the training I received at a younger age when it came to leadership and functionality. Capacity wise, I can handle it. But on the other hand, it is also about replenishing my energy. So I do have my own systems in place in terms of how I heal, recover, source my energy and myself so that I can continue to put on a good fight.

Nicole

It's really important to have a toolbox, or a bag of tricks, to maintain our own personal mental health. I like the word you used—*replenish* our energy.

MK

I can appreciate what you shared with me about the journey you went through. It wasn't all smooth. It took ups and down before you found what mattered to you and why you do what you do. That's why even though six years have passed, it doesn't feel that long. It's your calling.

Nicole

I find that it's similar to your journey too—passion and paying it forward. It's true that stigma is an issue, and there's a lot of struggle involved. But one thing I've uncovered is that there are a lot of good people that come into your life who impart their gifts to you, and you just can't help but want to pay it forward and make life just that little bit better for the next person.

CHAPTER 7

Self-Connection is the Prerequisite for Human Connection

By Simone Heng, Human Connection Speaker

Simone lost her father to cancer when she was nineteen, and her mum became paralysed when she was twenty-nine. However, in a stereotypically Asian way, she was taught to not grieve, but instead to move on and be strong. Eventually, she reached a breaking point when she was in a toxic work environment, and finally sought out a therapist where she had to confront the backlog of grief and trauma within her. She shares the importance of connecting with our emotions, even the difficult ones, as an important element of mental health and wellness.

CONNECTING WITH MYSELF AGAIN

MK

I'm very curious and interested to find out, how did you start doing what you do?

Simone

I dealt with a lot of trauma in my family from the time I was very young—something the therapist called little 't' trauma—through losing my dad to cancer when I was 19, and my mum becoming paralyzed when I was twenty-nine. There were a lot of things that were obviously affecting my mental health, but I didn't really have the self-connection to realize that these things were contributors. Being raised the Asian way, if someone passes away, even if you're young, you're taught to not grieve. Instead, you're taught to be strong, get over it and move on. So I pushed these hurts and pains deep down inside me and got disconnected from myself. And it got to a point where things started to get worse, especially when my mum became paralysed. If you don't process things, they just snowball.

I think the breaking point came for me when I moved back to Singapore in 2015 to a really toxic work environment. Whilst I was battling with my personal struggles, the lack of compassion, the lack of empathy, the stigmatization, and the bullying I received in the workplace compounded everything. It literally brought me to my knees. I was crying down the phone with my cousin. She's my best friend in the whole world. She's more like a sister, and she has been my rock. And when I lived in these different countries all over the world, she's the person I would call with my deepest darkest things. She has really seen me from birth all the way through. So I really trusted her when she said to me, with deep compassion, that 'You know babe, maybe you should talk to a professional'. And because it came from a place of somebody really knowing me and a place of deep respect and love—

[short pause]

Simone

It was the best thing that could have happened at that time. I remember talking to her a couple of weeks later after the first session with the counsellor and saying to her, 'Thank you so much, it was the best advice anyone's ever given me'.

I should say that the process of going to therapy when you have a backlog of grief and trauma is really confronting. First, it's really, *really* hard work. I realize that's why a lot of people avoid it. You are pulled inside out.

Now, Singapore doesn't offer subsidies for therapy. My uncle, who is a Singaporean migrant in Perth, reminded me that it's covered in Australia. I would have spent about SGD$20,000 on my own therapy, not subsidized, and it changed my life. It did start me thinking, if you don't have that money, what do you do to have this life changing experience?

But what we're really looking at is this whole arc about self-connection. If you don't have self-connection, which is knowing what you're feeling, when you're feeling it, and why you're feeling it—then the process of getting to a happy place takes a lot longer. Initially, I didn't connect with myself. I pushed my feelings aside. I listened to all the aunties who told me to get over it, 'Your father died already, move on'—all this kind of harsh cultural commentary about processing grief and trauma, about the shame of even calling something trauma when it *is* trauma. All this stigma made the journey to get there so much longer than it had to be, and that's what got me thinking about this topic of human connection. Because when you become much better connected with yourself, you can articulate how you're feeling, when you're feeling it, why you feel it, you know when you're triggered, and you know the kinds of situations and people that trigger you. Once you know that, you can start connecting better with others. You can start connecting much more consistently with people because you are building trust and connection, because you're showing up consistently for people.

Dealing with mental health issues also allows us to heal and then become more others-driven. I was so entangled in my own situations that my cup didn't runneth over. If someone needed me, I could not be there for them because I was exhausted from battling my own journey. Great self-connection is the primary prerequisite for any great human connection. That's why when I speak about the topic of human connection, I focus on the intersection of mental health and the lack of human connection, as well as putting a cultural slant on what we call *relational loneliness* in the way we grew up in Asian culture, sometimes being told in families that *you don't belong* or *you are the black sheep*. This kind of stuff creates a lack of belonging in us that then manifests later in life in some other issues as well.

[short pause]

Simone

And I will add that, because of the journey that I was on, not only have I grown with the topic of human connection, but I come to the topic as a humble student of it. There were times in my life where I've made every mistake possible with human connection and seen the emotional repercussions of doing it wrong, which is why it has become easier for me to teach it to other people. Because I come from a place where I was deeply flawed at it, and of course I still make mistakes—but I get better with it all the time. I don't hold myself up as *the* human connection expert, but I specialize in this area and I'm always exploring it.

MK

Everything you've just said does show that you've really found your past and dealt with what was buried inside of you.

Simone

Absolutely. And when going for therapy becomes confrontational is when the therapist asks you to talk about how you grew up and the dynamics in your family. When my therapist said *okay, there's a lot of trauma there,* and she used that word . . . It was very confronting for me to say *I had trouble in my childhood.* But the thing is, most people have some level of small trauma in their childhood.

MK

We all have it.

Simone

We all do.

So the worst part of therapy is when it takes you all the way down, breaks you apart, then puts you back together. When I was down on my knees emotionally, my therapist asked, 'What do you want to get out of this?' And I said, 'I want to be one of those people where criticism falls like water off a duck's back'. For these people, thinking about their childhood doesn't make them tear up. For these people, there is no shame, and I think that it's great now, because I now consider myself one of those people. When someone criticizes me now, it no longer triggers something in me that is reminiscent of a childhood experience.

MK

You can see it and hear it for what it is, instead of reacting to it.

Simone

Exactly. Now it's like, *okay, aunty wants to give her opinion.* I'm respectful, but I'm not triggered to react. I'm not triggered to question my identity based on aunty's verbalizations.

The interesting thing is when I found my own power by coming out of this journey, I also get a lot less comments from aunties because I look powerful now. I don't look like the *xiao mei mei*[22] that you can go and just say these things to. I think that I now have a level of being a little bit more intimidating, which works in stopping those interactions happening in the first place. People don't think they can come and say 'Why do you live your life like that' or 'What is wrong with the pimples on your face?' I think that has all to do with internal work and the energy that you show up with. You're much more centred after you do the internal work.

A LIFE WELL LIVED IS A LIFE BUILT AROUND CONNECTION

MK

Nice.

So, Simone, you know—this is the thing that's happening. A lot of times, even if we are aware that our traumas are still there, even if we are aware that our past is still hurting us, oftentimes we are afraid to look into our truth. We spend our whole life chasing the external game, getting more money, getting a good job, getting a next house, always chasing after the next thing. But we don't even give space for ourselves to look inwards. Why do you think this happens to us?

Simone

Firstly, I have to say that a life well-lived is a life built around connection. I've spent more time than I think most thirty-somethings have in a nursing home, and I would sit there with my mum from morning to night.

I can tell you this. The last thing people at the end of their lives—when their spouses have passed away, when they're left in a nursing home facility—talk about is what job they worked or how many cars they had. They are literally waiting for a human

---

[22] Xiao Mei Mei: Mandarin Chinese for little girl

connection, for someone to visit them. That is what they pine for. My mother was blessed. She had many visitors because she planted good seeds of human connection during her life. If you spend your life investing in material things and chasing external validation, that is a life that I have seen to be empty when you come to the end of it, because your human connections are your legacy. That is how you're going to be remembered. You could be remembered as the guy who had a lot of money, but what does that do for your legacy unless you gave some of that money to help people? Your legacy is not fame or money. It's how that fame or money helped other people in a positive way. That's the foreground of my psychology on a life centred on human connection.

I think it's still prevalent in Singapore because of culture. I've seen a rejection of that in other countries to some extent. There was a time when everybody was posting possessions and pretending to own Louis Vuitton bags on Instagram, and people are rejecting that in recent times. I think people want something deeper and more authentic. People want to feel connected.

But we have an issue in Singapore because our ancestors were people who came fleeing famine from the South of China, so they came with a threat mindset. That is why your parents say 'Make sure you finish everything on your plate'. That has been passed down to us. It's in our blood, and when you come from a threat mindset, what makes you feel successful is when you have abundance. Brené Brown says the opposite to threat is not abundance, but having enough.

MK

Correct.

Simone

And looking abundant to other people in the community is important because we're all a bit *kiasu*[23], right? So it's held up

---

[23] Kiasu: Hokkien slang for grasping, selfish attitude

as the model. It's not just being quietly abundant and happy. It's about being abundant, and *everyone has to see that I'm abundant.* I think that cultural pressure, hopefully through the work that we do, will see an inflection point where it also breaks.

I observe social media a lot and I see how disconnected the digitally-reared generation under me is. They literally will say that their friends are people they have fun with, but it's normal that their friends will not be there with them when they're down. They know their friends will cancel on them if something better comes along. And this is where connection is going for that generation and it's extremely dangerous to our mental health. Studies show that life expectancy increases for people with strong social connections, which is defined as people who will loan you money if you're in a financial bind, or people you can call when you're having an existential crisis. So the definition of connection and the definition of friendship is in flux. And what we're going to see is a generation that has forgotten how to connect. That will create an impact on our mental health, and hopefully, it will bring people away from materialism, away from just having fun, and back to deep connection, which is a base level need for us.

I can't emphasize it enough that our brains are configured from the time we're in hunter-gatherer tribes and need connection. When we're not connected, things seem overwhelming. We're flooded by a fight or flight response. Our psychological safety is threatened, and that leads to anxiety, depression, life-shortening diseases, and the chronic release of cortisol. These are all directly related to mental health. That's my long-form way of saying that there's got to be a change in the culture. And we only change culture by speaking out and having the bravery to speak out.

WHAT DOES IT TAKE TO BE VULNERABLE?

MK

Very interesting. And it brings me to my next question. As you're working with people on the ground, what are some stigmas you've observed that stops people from seeking help, even if they know they need it?

Simone

So almost a year ago now, one of my mentors from when I lived in Dubai took his own life when he was in quarantine. We were all blindsided by it, even though there were few people who knew he was going through a rough patch in life. I beat myself up for a long time. I thought he didn't say anything to me because I looked up to him as a mentor, and I would not have been the person he could show his weaknesses to. I thought maybe a guy friend could've stepped in to intervene. But I talked over dinner to a group of men around his age recently, and they said *Simone, even if you had been his guy friend, he probably wouldn't have told you because as men, we're not raised to show our vulnerabilities and talk about these things.* There are certain structures in our society that stop people from feeling they can be vulnerable. Which is why I try to be so vulnerable with all of my content, to show people that vulnerability does not make you weak. Vulnerability takes bravery and strength. You're basically saying, *I'm going to be vulnerable, talk about these issues, and face rejection in the eyes—but I'm going to do it anyway, because it's going to encourage somebody else to feel comfortable speaking out.*

But if we look at how we are raised in an Asian household, you don't talk about death in the family. You don't talk about sadness in the family. You don't talk outside of the family about anything that would make the family lose face, so then where do you talk about it? Well, mum and dad don't talk about it, so where do you put it? You press it deep down inside yourself and hope that you've got good friends that you can be vulnerable with. People fear rejection should they espouse their deepest darkest thoughts. And that fear is so great that people would rather be swallowed by the darkness and take their life than to speak their truth. So that whole idea that self-disclosure is a weakness has to change in order for people to feel they have a safe space to speak out.

MK

Got it. How do you think we can break these patterns?

Simone

So as I mentioned before, we have to become comfortable disclosing. You don't have to do it on a public stage like me. Find a group of friends where you can have these dialogues with, not just people that you buy stuff off Taobao with. There's got to be deeper things binding you to people so that when you are in a vulnerable position, and you can't talk to your family or your partner, or you at least have a human in your orbit that you feel safe enough to go to. That person might not understand, but should be someone who can listen wholeheartedly.

I think that that's also easier said than done, because when you are in a really lonely state, your perception of threat is higher. So you may have friends who are genuinely there for you, but you perceive that they're not. So that's really, really difficult. This is also why I publicly share what I share in the hope that somebody in that position sees it and goes, *Hey look, this girl is talking about this stuff, I don't have to be ashamed of what I'm going through.* That may be something in their computes, that they're not alone in their experience. Not only does speaking up help to remove stigma, but you are also allowing other people to feel less alone and more connected.

THE KEYS TO UNLOCK SELF-CONNECTION

MK

How do you think people can connect more deeply with themselves? The different dynamics in our relationships and how we relate with other people is really a function of how we relate with ourselves. And these relational issues are what's stopping people from seeking help. So I'm just wondering, how can we deepen our relationship with ourselves so that our relationships with other people can deepen as well?

Simone

One of the things I always say to the women I work with is this idea of being busy to distract from having to self-reflect. That's what we do with our fragmented attention spans. In this day and age of completely compressed timelines, we are not sitting with ourselves. We are uncomfortable sitting with ourselves, but we *need* to sit with ourselves. There has to be moments of stillness so that when something rubs you the wrong way, you can understand what you're feeling, what you're triggered by, and what the trigger feels like. These are the keys that unlock self-connection with yourself. For me, when I feel triggered, I feel an emotion rising in my stomach like a white-hot rocket. Other people might feel it in the neck or somewhere in their body. When I feel that emotion in my stomach, I know I'm triggered by something that happened in my childhood. Honour that feeling. You have to learn to sit in the discomfort in order to find healthy ways to cope with the pain. If we don't sit in that discomfort, we tend to soothe ourselves with other things, like shopping, drinking or eating, just so we don't have to connect with ourselves.

I'm a big advocate for step number one—learning to sit with yourself and sticking with the pain. I think that that's one really good thing that came out of working at that toxic workplace. I was working crazy hours, and when I would come back to my house because I didn't have any energy to go out and socialize, I had to sit with those feelings. I would have a window of one to two hours to eat and then go back to do some other projects for them. It was in those windows that I realized that *you are pretending you're happy, but you are not happy*. Even if I were to think about my parents, I would not be able to hold back the tears, and that was a sign to me that there was a whole energy around this that was not processed yet. I had a client today who's going through a lot of similar things as I was, and the moment she said the words *my mother and my father,* tears would start rolling down. These things are markers. Our body is telling us what's happening within us. So that's the number one step, sit with yourself.

Number two—there are incredible resources out there. If you can't afford therapy, the self-help section of the bookstore is quite incredible, so you can go and have a look. And here's the thing: we feel happier when there's momentum, when we feel we're moving forward in life. Education allows us to feel like we're moving forward. So get some good self-development books, or check them out of the library if you're on a student budget. It doesn't have to be a full-fledged $250/hour therapy session. One of the reasons I've become a better human connector is by learning more about the science behind why I'm feeling the way I'm feeling. When you understand your feelings better, it really helps to get rid of the self-loathing of *oh, I have trauma, I have problems, why can't I just be happy and basic like everyone else?* Knowledge is power.

Step number three—check in with how you're feeling and don't take every bit of advice from everybody as the law on how you should feel. Start listening to your internal voice on how you should feel.

MK

Nice. Anything you would like to share to the general public about vulnerability?

Simone

Look, vulnerability is thrown around a lot. For me, self-disclosure comes first. Vulnerability comes second. Self-disclosure is the act of making the choice to have dialogue about deeper things when you're with your friends by disclosing more information.

We hate doing this as Asians because we've been taught to keep it all private.

But here's the thing: we don't get to vulnerability if there's no self-disclosure. So if you practice self-disclosure—and it can just be about something small like how stressed you're feeling—then somebody else can connect with you by sharing about their own situation and it builds organically. That's how connection builds until you get to a point where there's a really great trusted friendship where you can then be vulnerable.

We get to vulnerability starting with the small day-to-day acts of self-disclosure and making the choice to go deeper with our connections, even within our family. My mum now can talk to me about her grief, her pain, and our childhood. It's the most incredible thing, but it's taken years and a stroke to rewire her to be okay with that, and I think it's wonderful. But we could have had this relationship much earlier had there been less stigma around disclosing information about yourself.

A CONVICTION TO LIVE LIFE ON YOUR OWN TERMS

Si Qi

Your career path has been quite unconventional, at least, compared to most of us. I think a lot of people's internal expectations are very different from what is expected of them, even if it's something small like, *I just want to be in marketing and instead of finance*. What are your thoughts on how we can do something that really matters to us?

Simone

I think this is the idea of personal autonomy. From a very young age, I have suffered ostracization from my family, my parents, and judgement from my community on both sides of my family for pursuing a life of joy. And I have been very close with people who've pursued the traditional path, who reached the age of forty-five, fifty, and are deeply unhappy because by that time in their career path, pivoting is much more difficult. So even though I suffered for fifteen years and worked really hard for very little money, with that fifteen years behind me, I'm able to pivot and make a really good income doing what I love. That was always the goal, but there's this suffering that had to happen for me to get there—which I think most people are not willing to go through. And because they're already lukewarm about fighting for their dream life, it's so much easier for an aunty or a mother or an uncle or a sister to derail and dissuade them from that. So it starts with a conviction for living life on your own terms.

Another thing is . . . I was still not living with my parents when I started pursuing my passion. In Singapore, it's a lot harder because a lot of young people that I speak to live at home with their parents. I had met this young kid who wanted to set up a green non-profit. He would go out trying to network and come home only to have his ambitions criticised by his parents. I think when you live in that environment with your parents, it's obviously a lot harder to do. I had to leave the house in order to get out of the clutches of those expectations. So it starts from a devotion and passion to live life on your own terms—only then will it be easier for you to tune into your own voice and develop a great relationship with yourself.

Si Qi

Well, that's the hardest part—conviction. Being able to lead a fulfilling life and a life that is yours is very linked to mental health.

Simone

Absolutely. Let me read you a quote from Johann Hari, one of the thought leaders on depression. He said: 'The worst stress for people isn't having to bear a lot of responsibilities. It's having to endure work that is monotonous, boring, soul-destroying, where they die little when they come to work each day because their work touches no part of them that is them'.

The work touches no part of you that *is* you! Oh my god, yes. Do you think it's linked to mental health?! And you think that doing a job you hate is linked to a disconnection with yourself? It is!

Si Qi

Totally.

Simone

Yeah, and if you just read Bronnie Ware's *The Top Five Regrets of the Dying*—

MK

I always talk about her stuff!

Simone

Yeah! So the number one regret of the dying was that they lived a life for other people, and not themselves. They lived a life that wasn't true to themselves.

You need to be audacious enough to want more for yourself. You don't want to get to the stage where you crystallise those limiting beliefs, that you believe you don't deserve better. So whatever you do now in your twenties, you are setting the paradigm for the rest of your life. And maybe that is the blessing in my trauma, that I got to see my dad die in front of me working seven days a week for twenty years to secure our family residency in Australia and never see his retirement. When you are a little girl and you see that, the message is pretty clear—retirement is not guaranteed for you. And secondly, why is everyone so scared to want more for themselves? That's cultural for us—that it's arrogant to think we should want more. *Who do you think you are, to want more than what your parents did?* So have the audacity to want more for yourself and then slowly go out and do it.

I would say that purpose is often linked to being of service. When we're of service to people, it reminds us that we're part of a bigger tribe and that we're connected. So if you're confused about your purpose, think about how you could be of service to the community. You'll find that if you're guided by that, you get much closer to finding that sweet spot of what you should be doing, and how you can build that into something that earns revenue.

MK

Thank you. That was very powerful.

CHAPTER 8

The Responsibility of Educating Yourself

By Jamie, Caregiver, Caregivers Alliance Limited

Jamie's sister was first diagnosed in 1997 with depression, and later diagnosed with paranoia schizophrenia. Jamie decided to care for her sister as she felt that it was her duty and responsibility to do so. She shares her struggles of finding balance to care for sister, while managing her own life and career as well. It is a daily negotiation that she finds herself in these twenty odd years of caring for her sister, and shares some of the support and resources caregivers can go to when they need help.

CAREGIVING IS A DUTY, NOT AN OBLIGATION

MK

I want to get to know you a little bit better in terms of what you do. What made you decide to do what you do today as a caregiver?

Jamie

My sister is not well, and I think it's my duty and responsibility as a sister to take care of another sister because I love her. It's not my occupation. My occupation is the head of strategy for a global digital company.

MK

What was it like for you, balancing these different roles and tasks?

Jamie

It's tough to have a black and white understanding about how much time needs to be negotiated on a weekly or daily basis to take care of my sister's needs, as well as to really give myself towards my career. I'm really trying to build myself up as well because you're only young once, and this is the time to grow your career. But a lot of it also . . . A lot of time was spent taking my sister in and out of IMH, in and out of hospitalizations, psychiatrists, psychologists, and different interventions that are available in Singapore to rehabilitate her back into the working world, which has not been successful. So I think understanding the balance between those two worlds is something that . . . There's no fixed rule. It's a daily negotiation with myself.

MK

Got it. When did you start becoming a caregiver? When did your sister have the issue?

Jamie

My sister was first diagnosed in 1997 from depression. She attempted suicide a few times.

[short pause]

Jamie

She attempted suicide a few times, and it's been ongoing from there. It's been ongoing from different variations, and different signs and symptoms of mental health issues that she has faced to the point now, where she is officially diagnosed with having paranoia schizophrenia.

MK

Got it.

[silence]

MK

This is where I'm gonna come from . . . I want to get to know the world of a caregiver inside out. What made you decide to do so on a personal level? Because you could actually hire a caregiver.

Jamie

Hiring a caregiver is for physical ailments and functionalities and operational functionalities. When I say operational functionalities, what I mean is, somebody to monitor the medication, make sure she's taking her injections, make sure that she has some company going into the doctor's appointments. I feel that those things you can hire a caregiver for, but anyone who understands mental health also understands that these issues are not functional and operational. Anyone suffering from a mental health issue is living in a highly subjective world where every day could be different. Temperaments could be different, whether you're talking about autism, schizophrenia, or dementia. The level of volatility in our loved ones' behaviours on a day-to-day basis can manifest very differently, and anybody that I know who's a caregiver for a loved one with a mental health condition automatically gets very concerned about their loved ones' disease or illness or condition. So there's absolutely no one that I know of, including myself, that can isolate themselves from caregiving and say *I'll just get a caregiver.*

IS THERE ANY END IN SIGHT?

MK

What are some of the issues and challenges caregivers often face?

Jamie

I can't speak on behalf of other caregivers, but the challenges and the issues that we face are balancing the various aspects of our own personal life and meeting the needs of our loved ones. And in our own personal life, it can be balancing time spent with our friends, our own free time, our own career growth, things that give us a sense of autonomy, and balancing the responsibility of caregiving for a loved one who's suffering from very, *very* ambiguous conditions which you know there's no cure for. Which leads me to one of the most important things – the trajectory of our caregiving responsibilities.

If you're a parent, the trajectory is that *I'm gonna care-give for my son and daughter.* Normal son-daughter, whatever normal is. But the caregiving journey between the parent and normal child is between the ages of zero and eighteen. After eighteen, they pretty much grow up and become adults. But for the trajectory for a caregiver towards someone who's suffering from mental health conditions, there's no end in sight. There is no way, somebody, a psychiatrist, a psychologist, or a doctor, can come to you and say, *Jamie, just give these five years of your time, and in five years she'll be fine.* So I think that the unknown trajectory of the fact that there's no end in sight, makes a lot of caregivers that I've spoken to feel like *when is this going to stop?* When is my loved ones' mental health condition going to get better? Sometimes it feels like it's never gonna get better. So how do you manage your own emotions? It's like a cycle. *How long is this gonna last? I don't know.* The signs and symptoms get worse. Your motivation goes down because you *FEEL* nothing you do is truly helping your loved one get better. Sometimes you want to give up. You reach the burnout. When you reach the burnout, who and what are the resources that you can tap into that can help you bounce back and go through the cycle?

MK

So it's really about finding out what recharges you and sources you as well.

Jamie

Yes, yes.

[silence]

MK

How's your sister now?

Jamie

There are ups and there are downs. There are good days and there are bad days. She's okay for now.

MK

Got it. And the condition started in 1997?

Jamie

The mental health illness diagnosed as depression at that time started in 1997, yes.

MK

Got it. Got it. I don't know whether this is sensitive to ask or not—

Jamie

Yep.

MK

It's been more than twenty years already?

Jamie

Yeah, twenty-three I think. Twenty-four?

[short pause]

Jamie

What's your question?

MK

It's difficult to put together the question, but you know—

Jamie

I'll help you, don't worry.

[short pause]

MK

I felt that you know, you must have . . . Were there days where you felt resigned?

Jamie

Yeah, I think that happens with life in general. But with this particular illness, it's never getting better. And that's why I brought up the cycle just now where you feel the signs and symptoms are getting worse no matter what you do. So your motivation goes down. That's where resignation seeps in.

MK

How do you pick yourself up?

Jamie

It goes back to finding the resources you're willing to tap into that can help you out.

Now, what do I mean by resources? One is the practical resources. There are government agencies, nonprofit, charitable organizations, etc. The practical things that you need, the tools that you need to pick yourself up. And then there are other things that I would feel, if you're an older caregiver like me, forty years and above, there's a certain sense of understanding yourself, your inner self. What picks me up? I know exercises that pick me up. I know what kind of foods to eat just to indulge in a little bit of self-pleasure. So you put aside whatever is happening right now with your loved ones and try to focus on some me-time. Even if it's just a few minutes a day, find something to focus on that helps you recharge and rejuvenate.

There's a psychiatrist who taught me, 'Jamie, try to find some time to discuss this either internally with yourself, either with a counsellor, or either with your other family members maybe once or twice or week'. *Don't worry yourself all the time about this.* So park some time aside each week that you can truly attribute towards problem solving, so that you don't have the guilt and the shame of not doing enough, not paying attention, that you're not able to balance whatever your loved one needs in terms of attention, in terms of medication, in terms of health, in terms of rehabilitation. Box this aside as something that you understand you need to deal with, but maybe not right now. Maybe set aside one hour every Tuesday to talk about it. Maybe set aside one hour every Wednesday, and the rest of the time, take care of yourself, and like I said, taking care of yourself means practical tools. Understanding some sort of self-indulgence that you can participate in. For me, that means going out with my friends. That means having once a week where I can really forget about everything and spend one whole day, like a Saturday, out enjoying myself with friends. Sunday is family day. Monday is work day. Tuesday is where we sit down and talk about a step-by-step structure, a step-by-step process as to how we can deal with my sister's condition. Wednesday is again back to work. So every Tuesday for me is problem-solving time. That helps me regain some balance.

INFORMATION, INFORMATION, INFORMATION!

MK

Okay, let's look at three different perspectives. From the individual perspective of a caregiver, from a collective as a society, then in terms of policymakers. What are some interventions, in your opinion, that can be done more or better in the current situation and state that we're in?

Jamie

From a caregivers' perspective, I believe there's a lot of resources out there. I believe they don't have to be local resources all the time, but they can be resources available from other countries such as Australia, who is doing a lot on mental health and they have a lot of research to back up what youth mental health might be, what adult mental health might be. There are *TONS* of resources available on Google and books available for free in Singapore libraries that give us concrete knowledge about mental health and clarify some myths we may have. There was a doctor once who told me, *you can't fight what you don't know.* For caregivers, we have a certain sense of helplessness that we feel. It's innate, and we feel *I don't know what's going on,* there's a loss of control, *I don't know how to help myself, I don't know how to help my loved one.* And I don't think we can operate with a sense of sensibility from a state of helplessness and fear. So one of the doctors shared with me, you know Jamie, *go out there, get information. You may not get all your answers right now, but it's not about finding the answers. It's about slowly gathering information that will make you feel more in control of the situation.* That has helped.

On a policy level, whenever I make comparisons, I'm very empathetic because I know what the system was twenty years ago. So when I talk about it, I don't talk about it with the blindsight that the government is not doing anything to help. Yes, more needs to and can be done to provide more accessibility to mental health care in Singapore, but we have come a long way from that of twenty years ago. Let me start off by first saying I'm grateful for the evolution that has happened in twenty years in Singapore when it comes to making mental health a priority. But, there is much to be done because we don't have enough clarity and understanding with regards to what mental health resources are available for caregivers and their loved ones. It is also with regards to capability-building for rehabilitation, and also, making mental health education a priority in schools so that students can develop a strong understanding of their mental health needs. Another ambiguous area is getting insurance policy issues for our loved ones. No insurance agency is willing to cover or provide my sister with insurance coverage for hospitalization, infectious disease, chronic disease, and more, just because she has had mental health issues for some time now. I really think this is discrimination against those who have mental health conditions, and we must find a way around this with private insurance companies.

Now, I think the training and rehabilitation services in the government's ecosystem that are available are *AMAZING* compared to what they were even five years ago. These services are being inundated at the moment as we speak. So I think where areas can be improved is to democratize these services to communities within Singapore so that it doesn't just isolate itself into IMH or NUH[24] which are the two most equipped hospitals

---

[24] NUH: National University Hospital

to help with mental health conditions. But the other areas, the family centres, are stepping up—and that's one thing I really appreciate. There are other community centres, nonprofit, rehab centres that are all stepping up, but I feel they are all overwhelmed at the moment due to the sudden increase of patients suffering from mental health challenges during COVID. In Singapore, I feel there's a lack of mental health professionals, from doctors, to nurses, to medical social workers. I feel like the industry itself is being overloaded because there is just not enough talent and resources at the moment. Not because the government doesn't want to do anything—we just don't have enough psychologists, psychiatrists, nurses, and healthcare professionals across a spectrum of diseases, to truly be allocated on a ratio that helps in making sure that people in Singapore are being well taken care of, because there's only so much that the government can do.

MK

Got it. Now, if there's a message you want people out there to hear, what would that be?

Jamie

As clinical as this may sound, it's *information. Information, information, information.* Go out there, try to seek to understand, and try not to judge. It's easier said than done because as human beings, to judge is so intuitive. Everyone does it. But I think truly, if there's a friend or a family member of yours who's suffering from a mental health condition, or that you suspect may be suffering, go online, *read, read, read,* before you attempt to rationalize and judge. Because what's happening out there is that many people read one or two articles and think that they understand everything about mental health, and then they start diagnosing their friends.

MK

Yes!

Jamie

And I really feel that that is a very, very, very *dangerous* path that we are walking on, because a lot of young people who are thirty years old, twenty years old, are attempting to diagnose their friends after reading one book, one article, one magazine. They think they have enough information to make that judgement. I think that's *INCREDIBLY* dangerous because not only do they think that they're equipped to diagnose someone, but their judgement follows, and that judgment doesn't help. But empathy does. So seek to understand and practice empathy, not judgement.

CHAPTER 9

Mental Health Recovery is Possible

By Deborah Seah, Founder, Community of Peer Support Specialists (CPSS)

Deborah was admitted to IMH in 2016, and in that same year, her psychiatrist connected her to a peer support specialist as Deborah displayed the attributes needed to become one. In 2018, Deborah founded the Community of Peer Support Specialists advance the peer support movement in Singapore. She recounts her mental health journey, the challenges she faced with stigma, and how she found hope for recovery and purpose in her journey.

MAKING SENSE OUT OF MY PAIN AND SUFFERING

MK

Could you share with us the work that you do?

Deborah

Sure. Apart from my full-time job, I have a vocation as a certified peer support specialist. That is something that I do on a voluntary basis. How it all started was when my psychiatrist connected me to a peer support specialist at IMH in 2016 because she saw, in me, the attributes needed to become one. She told me that I have resilience and I take personal responsibility for my recovery. I was invited to attend a Recovery and Wellness Sustenance Workshop which we call RWS, in short, and I completed all nine sessions of the workshop and graduated with a certificate. That prepared me to be enrolled in a course to receive the Peer Support Specialist (PSS) certification. After I graduated in March 2017, I became a certified peer support specialist and I started my vocation in this field.

I did my practicum at Caregivers Alliance, which is an organization I currently still volunteer at to share my recovery story in both the English and Chinese classes for the caregivers. I was also a paid peer support specialist in the mood disorder unit at IMH from April to September 2017 for about six months. Then in August 2017 I started volunteering at this charity organization called PSALT Care, which is a mental health agency that supports persons in recovery from mental health conditions and addiction issues and I'm currently still a support group facilitator there. I have a PSS Train-the-Trainer certificate and I graduated from the pioneer batch. I'm involved in the training of the peer support specialists in the subsequent runs and I actually just completed the training of the sixth batch last week.

Apart from that, I founded a Community of Peer Support Specialists (CPSS) in December 2018 where I gathered the alumni of the PSS training, and we come together to ground ourselves in peer support principles and to advance the peer support movement in Singapore. So yeah, that's some of the stuff that I do.

MK

Got it. Could you share more about why you wanted to become a peer support specialist?

Deborah

Well, I was admitted into IMH in 2016. I read this book in the ward called *The Purpose Driven Life* written by Rick Warren. I was at the lowest point of my life and when I read the book, I suddenly felt that I could make some sense out of my pain and my suffering. That was when I felt a passion and a burden to explore deeper the purpose of having mental health challenges. And when I met a peer support specialist, everything just connected, you know. I just felt very inspired, because it never occurred to me that recovery could be possible. Initially I felt that I was going to be on medication for life, going to be like my aunties and uncles, because mental illnesses run in my paternal family. It's genetic. Meeting the peer support specialist gave me hope and it sparked off a desire in me that I wanted to be like him, who is my role model, my mentor. So I started contributing in small ways and giving back to society, and that's how my passion grew.

Si Qi

If we could just backtrack a little bit—

Deborah

Sure.

Si Qi

What actually pushed you to embark on your mental health recovery? What was the process like?

Deborah

I started having symptoms when I was in lower primary. I was suicidal, I had a lot of symptoms, and I was just grappling with them, but it just didn't occur to me that it could be a mental illness. Even though it was running in my family, I think I just couldn't accept it, you know, even when I started showing the symptoms and I was really struggling. Even when I entered society to work, I was fighting my fluctuating energy levels, because I'm actually a person in recovery from bipolar disorder and generalized anxiety disorder, so there were these highs and lows that were really hard to manage. I would be on medical leave from time to time, and my body system would just shut down. So that was really hard, grappling with managing a job. I think I was almost a 'crippled' person, yet not being able to disclose it because of the stigma.

Si Qi

Were you aware that it was bipolar disorder and anxiety at that time?

Deborah

At that time, I wasn't aware yet. In fact, I only came to realize it when I hit my rock bottom, when I had postnatal depression, and that was the time when it affected my functionality. I was just sleeping throughout the weekend, you know. I couldn't even upkeep my hygiene when I used to be very particular about cleanliness. My ex-husband was really concerned because my family couldn't manage me anymore. So that was the point where he brought me to IMH. We went to a polyclinic to get a referral and then I started seeing a psychiatrist in IMH. That was when my recovery journey began.

Si Qi

Right, okay. So now, you've found your purpose in trying to help people as a peer support specialist. Could you tell me a little bit more about how this purpose strengthens you? What makes you feel connected to this purpose?

Deborah

I guess there is a lot of fulfilments and meaning that I find as I share my recovery story on different platforms. Each time I share it, I feel that it's very refreshing. It's a reminder of how far I have come, and it makes me feel very grateful that I have progressed thus far even though I was on the verge of giving up, of ending it all back then. And it gives me that motivation to continue to sustain my wellness and to stay well because I know that I have peers and people looking up to me as a role model of recovery, so I have to keep going. These are the things that drive me. Also, knowing what it is like to have struggled in silence for more than two decades and then finally seeking help, I advocate for early intervention.

COMING TO TERMS WITH MY MENTAL HEALTH

Si Qi

What were the biggest stigmas that you faced when dealing with your mental health?

Deborah

The personal stigma for me was that I just couldn't accept that I would need to be on medication. Medication was a mental block for me because I'm the kind of person who would not even take Panadol when I have a headache, you know. I would just *tahan*.[25] So when I knew that *oh it's a chemical imbalance in my brain and*

---

[25] Tahan: Malay slang for tolerate

I need to be on medication, that was something I couldn't accept, that I would have to rely on medication. And when I went for the Recovery and Wellness Sustenance Workshop, there was a topic on medication and it was an eye-opener to me. I realized that *oh, actually, what's wrong with taking medication?* People with diabetes need to be on insulin. People with asthma need to be on Ventolin. And if you have a chemical imbalance in the brain, then you take psychiatric medication. So I realized that *oh, actually, it's no big deal.* That was when I became more open towards that. I realized through medication, when it stabilized my mood, that I was able to have a job, contribute to society, and enjoy that quality of life. I think in terms of external stigma, when I started going to IMH for appointments, I would take a taxi or Grab, and the drivers would say *oh, you going to IMH? Are you a patient there?* And I just felt that the drivers gave a kind of look and stigmatized me. And I would feel very ashamed. I would be very affected and when I came back from my appointment I would just cry. I would tell my ex-husband that I hated it, that I just couldn't accept it, and it lingered for some time. I think the turning point was after I became a certified peer support specialist. I became more ready because I felt that I had gotten over that self-stigma, that regardless of how people looked at me and all, I didn't feel affected anymore and in fact, I would even use my Grab rides to educate them. When they ask *are you going to IMH?* I would say *oh yes, yes I'm going there.* I mean when they look at me, maybe because I'm well-dressed and all, they would wonder, *huh you're a patient there?* And I'll say *oh yes, I'm going for my appointment*, or *I'm going down to visit friends*, and if they have some comments or anything, I end up educating them, so it no longer affects me anymore.

Si Qi

And in your work as a peer support specialist, what kind of stigmas do you see in the community?

Deborah

Society generally views my peers as unpredictable, irresponsible, or even lazy. Some even deem us as dangerous, and then I realized that usually no employer will dare to hire someone with a mental health condition if there are better candidates because they might see a person in recovery as a liability to the company. So these are some of the things I sense from the ground and through what my peers share in the support group sessions, these are also the struggles they face in society.

Si Qi

Right. You were saying that you had a really hard time accepting that you needed to get professional help, or for your case, take medication. I think that's something a lot of people struggle with as well. There is this self-stigma that people have that is separate from the stigma that other people may have, in that you yourself cannot accept this reality that has dawned upon you.

Deborah

Yeah, you'll be in a state of denial and reckoning. I think one main hurdle was I couldn't take the step forward because I didn't want to have a record in IMH which I thought would taint my record. I would not be able to get a job in the public sector and it was going to stick with me for life. But right now, I think there are a lot of options available where they can see a GP in private.

MY CONDITION DOES NOT DEFINE MY DESTINY

Si Qi

How did you overcome that personal stigma or personal struggle to get help?

Deborah

I guess it is knowing my identity. Knowing that my diagnosis doesn't define my identity. It's like bipolar disorder and Deborah is separate, you know? I have this condition, but it is a condition that is up to me to manage, and it's not going to define my destiny. Which is why as a Beyond the Label campaign ambassador, my slogan is *my mental health condition does not limit my potential.* I actually received a ten-year Long Service Award when I was working in a tertiary institution despite being undiagnosed back then.

The process of getting help wasn't easy, but I would say that support and assurance from my family was very important. Seeing that my family members and my loved ones were affected when I was sad, when I felt very useless, and when I just gave up my hope in life—that was something that really propelled me forward. I think that hurt them badly, and one thing that they told me, and it means something very deep to me and impacted me a lot, was that they just want me to be happy. Doesn't matter whether I can work or not, they just want me to be happy. And I realized that my happiness is tied to their happiness, so I have to be happy. That actually gave me strength.

MK

It motivates you.

Deborah

Yes, it motivates me to accept my condition and to move on and to find meaning out of it.

Si Qi

How would you encourage somebody if they're struggling with accepting their diagnosis?

Deborah

I would want them to know that recovery is possible for everyone. This is my firm belief. Everybody may recover at a different pace because everybody has their own time. You never know when that AHA! moment would come, when the turning point would be, so do not give up and just keep trying, keep exploring options. You never know what you may discover that might work for you. Like flowers, we bloom in different seasons. So there is a time for everyone. That time will come, so long as they don't give up hope.

IT TAKES A COMMUNITY OF WELLNESS TO RECOVER

Si Qi

Nice!

So at ThisConnect, sometimes we run webinars where we engage different speakers to talk about mental health. And I remember very clearly there was this one question an audience member raised about what we can do to advise somebody who feels resigned because they've been to a psychologist, a psychiatrist, and they feel like that didn't help them. And I think that's the feeling that some people feel, which is that *I go for therapy, counselling, but I don't feel any better, my life hasn't changed.* So then they give up, they just stop on their recovery journey. Do you see that a lot in the mental health space? What does recovery really look like?

Deborah

I'm very fortunate because my psychiatrist is very good. I had a good rapport with her and she could really understand my struggles. There is that personal touch. I do know that there are some people who cannot really click with the psychologist, and having that trust and rapport is very important. You have to feel that your psychiatrist is really, really concerned and is really serious about your treatment plan and all. I have heard of many people who feel that, *oh, seeing a psychiatrist and going for psychotherapy, going for counselling, nothing works*. But one thing I would recommend to them is this, 'Would you like to explore attending a peer support group?' Because for me, peer support was actually a key component in my recovery.

Many of my peers realize that they are not alone in their struggles after attending a peer support group. I think this is a very important point to know that *hey, there are so many like-minded people going through the same struggle and we're accompanying one another on this journey*. I think that itself gives us a lot of strength.

No man is an island. It takes a community of wellness to recover together. And they will feel that they are empowered with a recovery culture and with a conducive environment. So this is something that I would introduce to them because this is my passion. It is why I started the Community of Peer Support Specialists, wanting to advance the peer support movement in Singapore, wanting to integrate this peer support discipline into the system. And I would say that all, if not most of them, will keep coming back, and they would be attached with the community and start to make progress in their recovery.

Si Qi

What does the peer support group do, and how does it help people in their recovery journey?

Deborah

In the peer support group that I facilitate at PSALT Care, we are grounded on the concept of WRAP®, which stands for Wellness Recovery Action Plan. I think it's very important because with WRAP®, they will develop their daily maintenance plan, something that is fairly essential to maintaining a person's wellness. So at least we don't just talk about things in the air you know. We talk about practical actions.

There are five key concepts of recovery: Hope, Personal Responsibility, Education, Self-advocacy and Support, so we draw on that concept and rotate each concept on a monthly basis. And we also have sharing sessions on particular topics where peers will share their perspective and lived experiences. There are also recreational activities, like hiking and art classes.

MK

So it's really a social community ecosystem that supports one another.

Deborah

Yes, right.

HOLDING THE HOPE

MK

Great. If there's a message that you could send out to the world about mental health, what would that be?

Deborah

There is this phrase that I learnt in my course called *holding the hope*. And even the book that we published through CPSS is based on this title. I would encourage everyone, even if you don't have a mental health condition, to hold the hope for your loved ones or your friends and even other people who are battling a mental health challenge. To hold the hope for them to know that recovery is possible. I think that is a very important point because when a person becomes resigned to fate or loses that motivation in life, it's because they lose hope. They feel that the future is just bleak.

Hope is very important. It's fundamental in recovery and it's something that I hold fast to, even at times when I'm tired in my recovery. As long as there is someone else holding the hope for another person, I think that gives the person strength to move on.

MK

And who was the beacon of hope for you during your time?

Deborah

It was my psychiatrist. She was really that beacon of hope. And she continues to be that beacon of hope. Even when I brought CPSS to an international conference, when I was sharing my recovery story in the workshop, she was there among the audience listening to my recovery story and she was on the verge of tears. I think that is something beyond my imagination, to meet my psychiatrist at an international conference on Together Against Stigma (TAS) I was speaking at. Of course, my loved ones as well, my mom who is my caregiver, my brother and sister. They have all been very supportive.

CHAPTER 10

Taking the First Step to Seek Help

By Nadera Binte Abdul Aziz, Peer Support Specialist, Community of Peer Support Specialists (CPSS)

Nadera struggled with her own mental illness for almost ten years before she got diagnosed and started taking medications. In 2014, after graduating from university, with the support and encouragement of those around her, she began to share her story in hopes that it might help someone else. That was the beginning of her advocacy journey. When she found CPSS, she naturally signed up for it as there is no end to the knowledge of helping another person.

UNDERSTANDING AND ACCEPTING A DIAGNOSIS

MK

First of all, I'd like to understand, what made you decide to become a peer support specialist?

Nadera

I struggled with my own mental illness for almost ten years before I got diagnosed and started taking medication. In 2014, after graduating from university, with the support and encouragement of those around me, I began to share my story in hopes that it might help someone else. That was the beginning of creatingsmiles, the Facebook page where I talk about mental health and my lived experiences, and my advocacy journey. When I heard about the peer support specialist programme by NCSS[26] and IMH, naturally I signed up for it, because I don't think there's an end to the knowledge about how to help someone.

MK

What were some of the struggles you experienced while walking on this path?

Nadera

The first time I saw a professional was when I was Primary 5, so I was ten. I initiated to see my school counsellor because I was having suicidal ideations and stress due to pressure from school and my family. I did not inform my family about it. I am really proud of my younger self who had enough self-awareness and courage to seek professional help. After years of therapy, I only sought a diagnosis when I was nineteen. So from ten to nineteen years old, it was a lot of just trying to understand what was wrong

---

[26] NCSS: National Council of Social Service

and seeing various counsellors to cope and get through my major exams with acceptable grades. There weren't any talks in schools about mental health, so I did all the research on my own. Despite sharing about the struggles I was going through, because I was still able to function well in school, counsellors often assumed me to be doing fine as I was not meeting the stereotypical idea of someone with depression. When I was nineteen, I found a youth mental health service called CHAT[27] that offered a free mental health check for youths aged sixteen to thirty so I went, was referred to IMH for treatment, and got my diagnosis.

Since then, of course my symptoms and challenges have evolved, unfortunately for the worse. But I strive to stay on course; to continue reaching out for help, to take my medication, and receive therapy.

MK

What mental health conditions were you assessed to have?

Nadera

When diagnosed at nineteen, I was assessed to have clinical depression. To date, I still have depression, but also borderline traits and dissociative traits which are largely seen in people with trauma. So uncovering that trauma to understand how everything started is what I am working on with my medical team.

MK

Got it. How has it been for you?

Nadera

Frankly, it's been very difficult. But I guess with all diagnoses, at the onset it's hard to accept, and there might be confusion here

---

[27] CHAT: Community Health Assessment Team

and there. The difference is that before my first diagnosis, I spent so much time trying to understand what was going on that when I was actually diagnosed with depression, I was relieved because I finally could have a name to it. I finally knew what's going on and that I could do something about it.

Whereas now, I have lots of grey areas and memory lapses, and with trauma work there is an overhaul of dissociations, emotions, and memory flashes. If you do not see a therapist trained in trauma work, you can regress and relapse or even suffer additional trauma. I had that experience, which made seeking help difficult at first, because I wasn't sure I could feel safe enough with my therapist. Thankfully, I am in good hands.

Majority of the people with trauma will attest that it is very challenging and takes time. To me, it's like opening a can of worms—the worms being all the stuff you've been suppressing all these years, or memories your brain repressed. My mind and body are just in chaos, but I know I have to keep at it to move forward in my recovery. So it's been very emotional, very confusing, very chaotic. The support of my medical team, my friends, and my family helps me to just hang on and trust the process.

UNDERSTANDING AND ACCEPTING A DIAGNOSIS

MK

What is it like living with these conditions and going public with your experience?

[Nadera laughs]

Nadera

Well, I think Singapore has come a long way from ten years ago in public awareness of mental health and accepting people with mental health conditions. We have nation-wide public education campaigns like 'Beyond the Label'. Schools have talks on mental health. There is even consideration of including it into the student curriculum. Tertiary institutions have a peer support programme where interested students are trained to offer support to other students and to promote wellness. We have Peer Support Specialists working in various settings showing that we can effectively work and contribute like everyone else. However, we cannot stop our collective efforts. A recent study by IMH showed that there's still a large percentage of people who still have misconceptions of what mental health is, who still think that people with mental health conditions are dangerous people or people they will not work or live with. I want to keep advocating so that ten years later, everyone's efforts collectively contribute to a kinder, less-stigmatized and more inclusive Singapore. I was personally inspired by advocates who shared their experiences ten years ago when stigma was much stronger. And I saw the huge impact that was made in programmes and services being offered, and even policy changes. I am not rich, business-minded, or someone capable of running my own start up. What I have though, is my story and my voice. I think sharing my story is a powerful way for me to spread the message. Through this I've also met a lot of other advocates as well, so it's been very heartening. I don't feel like I'm doing this alone because I know there are other advocates who are my friends now, who are trying to do their part.

Of course, with the day-to-day condition . . .

[Nadera laughs]

Nadera

It's a . . . It's a learning process. Recovery is not linear. There are ups and downs, of course. And maybe because of this new diagnosis and these new symptoms that are coming up for me, there have been more downs than ups. With depression, I think it was a lot easier to understand. It was also more straightforward for my family to understand. But with my current new diagnosis, it's more complex. Even I am struggling to understand it, so what more can I expect from my family? What I do is actively expand my support system. I've been attending more support groups where I can share my struggles and hear others share theirs and what helps them. When being part of such groups where members have similar struggles, there is a unique healing and therapeutic effect that allows me to feel safe and be less isolated.

PEOPLE WITH MENTAL HEALTH CONDITIONS CAN CONTRIBUTE TO THE COMMUNITY

MK

Is there a message from your personal journey that you wish to share with the public?

Nadera

Peer support specialist practice in Singapore is still in its stage of infancy. I think many people, including mental health professionals, don't know about us and what we do.

To me, peer support specialists exemplify that those with lived experiences in mental health have something unique to give back that others who have not gone through this experience cannot. We journey with others who are going through their own mental health struggles using our experience. I hope this shows the public and employers that people with mental health conditions have strengths, can contribute to society, and are just like you and I. We are people who have a lot of empathy because we've been through a lot and can empathize with someone else.

For those who are struggling, my message would be that . . . It is very easy to ask someone to seek help, but actually going out there and seeking help can be a very scary thing. For me, I had to do it all by myself during the early years of my recovery as I didn't have any support. But once you overcome that barrier and you're connected to someone, that person will be able to help you and connect you to more support. Despite my struggles, I was high-functioning, but I experienced stigma and discrimination. Even mental health professionals didn't take my challenges seriously. I was told I was fine, that I just needed to relax and exercise. One even told me to do yoga and you'll be okay. And these are psychiatrists who meet many patients that depend on them for help. So if you also feel that something is not right, but at the same time you are still doing well in school or work, trust your gut. If your gut feeling says that something is not right, then something is probably not right no matter what your family, friends or counsellors think. And you may not get the right help at the get go. You may not have the best chemistry or understanding with the first psychiatrist or therapist you see. It is common, so don't give up or let a few bad experiences faze you. And finally, my message to the mental health professionals . . . Please do not underestimate, dismiss, or look down on the struggles of high-functioning individuals. There was a day I had a suicide plan and I walked into office knowing that it would be my last, but no one around me could tell, because of how well I masked it up.

SEEKING HELP CAN BE SCARY

MK

Thank you. That was very informative. I think it's going to create an angle and a direction to help people who are struggling to reach out. Is there anything else you wish to share with me?

Nadera

Increasingly, what I'm seeing is that more people know how and where to seek help, but they're scared and just need assurance. I think that's a good sign.

It's natural to have that hesitance or fear. 'What if that place doesn't work out for me? What if that place rejects me or doesn't take me seriously?' And I guess that's where your work will help. The putting together of different experiences so people get to hear from others that it's okay, it's safe, nothing bad is going to happen.

I think it's very important to keep spreading the message, to keep it active on everyone's radar about the different places they can go to seek help and to encourage more conversations surrounding mental health. When more people come out and share their personal experiences, more will feel encouraged, and hopefully then be able to overcome the fear of getting help. This is my personal view on what mental health awareness can work towards in Singapore in the coming years.

CHAPTER 11

Driven by Contentment

By Navin Amarasuriya, Director,
The Contentment Foundation Singapore

Navin previously worked in a luxury goods company, and he explains how the best customers were those who were never satisfied—they kept coming back for more. However, people who are stuck in the cycle of constantly chasing after objects may end up pursuing things that do not add to their wellbeing. Especially in a society like Singapore, where economic and consumer goals are of top priority, pursuing wellbeing could be antithetical to the goals of economic growth as one of the core concepts of fulling oneself is to understand that perhaps we are enough. Navin suggests some ways we pursue meaningful goals that bring contentment to us in the long run.

THE BEST CUSTOMERS ARE THE PEOPLE WHO ARE NEVER SATISFIED

Si Qi

Can you tell us more about yourself?

Navin

I was working in operations in a luxury goods company for many years and through that experience, I got to see people who are very wealthy and the objects that people pursued as they were seeking happiness. So the narrative is if you can afford these things, you've made it in life and therefore, theoretically, people who have the money to be able to consume this should be the happiest people in the world.

[short pause]

Navin

At least, that's what marketing tells us. But the reality is that the best customers we have are the people who are never satisfied. There's a concept in psychology called hedonic adaptation[28], which describes how people constantly change their goalposts after fulfilling a certain desire. For example, if you suddenly got upgraded to business class from economy class, you would be amazed by how spacious the seats are and how nice the food is. But the novelty wears off after a few times, and you adapt to this new state. It is a tendency of the human condition to not recognize what we already have. People who are stuck in the cycle of constantly chasing after objects may end up pursuing things that don't add to their wellbeing.

---

[28] Shane Frederick and George Loewenstein, 'Hedonic adaptation,' in Well-being: *The Foundations of Hedonic Psychology*, ed. Daniel Kahneman, Ed Diener, and Norbert Schwarz (New York: Russell Sage Foundation, 1999), 302–329

I think this happens a lot in Singapore where society can sometimes set us up to not look at what truly matters within us. When you think about the goals of growing an economy or growing a consumer base, it can sometimes be antithetical to the goals of wellbeing, because one of the core concepts of fulfilling oneself is to understand that perhaps we are enough.

It's interesting because Singapore talks a lot about innovation and creativity, but we don't talk about emotions like disappointment or sadness. The way we relate emotionally, can either cause us to give up, or give us meaning to stay curious and move forward. Thomas Edison, the inventor of the lightbulb, was once asked by a reporter 'How did it feel to fail 1,000 times?' Edison replied 'I didn't fail 1,000 times. The light bulb was an invention with 1,000 steps'. Social and emotional learning helps us to look at our emotional states and see that there are no real positive or negative emotions. Instead, each emotion has something valuable to teach us.

HOW MUCH MONEY IS ENOUGH?

Si Qi

We have been speaking to many people over the past month and the theme of wealth and how it doesn't necessarily fulfil the human soul keeps coming up. I want to know your thoughts about this. When you were working in the luxury goods company, what was it that money couldn't fulfil within people?

Navin

So there's actually a really famous study where researchers analyzed over 450,000 respondents and found out that while emotional wellbeing rises with income, it does not progress further beyond an annual income of roughly \$75,000.[29] The research defines

---

[29] Daniel Kahneman and Angus Deaton, "High Income Improves Evaluation of Life but Not Emotional Well-Being," *Proceedings of the National Academy of Sciences* 107, no. 38 (2010): 16489–93. doi:10.1073/pnas.1011492107

emotional wellbeing as the 'emotional quality of an individual's everyday experience'. Even though emotional wellbeing increases with income at the start, it doesn't mean that if you earned $300,000, you'd be four times as happy compared to when you were earning $75,000. And so there is a line between enough and too much. I think we all know that.

In Singapore, we've always been told this survival narrative, and that was true when we began our journey as a country. But I think we've not stopped to ask ourselves how much is enough as well. Growing economic capital is not necessarily a good or bad thing, but sometimes to grow that capital, we lose other kinds of capital, such as relationship capital. For instance, a successful business might have very strong financial capital, but if the ownership structure of the business is very weak, it can create instability for the management team, and that's where relationship capital, or lack thereof, comes into the picture. Relationship capital is important, but we need to invest in it, and that takes time and energy. Another type of capital is the health capital. We often read stories of people in very stressful professions who adopt unhealthy lifestyle habits to relieve stress, say drinking frequently, smoking or overeating, behaviours that ultimately have a negative impact on their health. There's that old saying right, that in our pursuit of wealth we ultimately end up spending that wealth on health.

And actually, the one currency we can't buy back is time. Imagine if we knew that this is the last year we're going to live, we'll probably think about our time very differently. So we have to balance the idea that while material wealth is important, there is a point when we have enough. And once we hit that point, then the question becomes *what can we do to improve our quality of life and wellbeing?* There's a really famous psychiatrist called Viktor Frankl who wrote a book called *Man's Search for Meaning*. There is a beautiful quote from the book where he said those who have a 'why' to live, can bear almost any 'how'. One of the lessons I took from that book was that happiness cannot be approached directly. It is a by-product of meaning. If you try to approach happiness directly, it becomes a hedonic adaptation problem where we try to optimize for something that we can never really arrive at. But if you're in pursuit of meaning, if you find the deeper *why* of why you exist and why you do what you do, then the act of working towards that meaning is a kind of happiness in itself.

GETTING THE FISH TO LOOK AT THE FISHBOWL

MK

I'm actually very curious. What inspired you to do the things that you do?

Navin

It's . . . I mean, wouldn't you do this? I don't know. No one wakes up in the morning saying *I want to suffer the whole day at work*. We work to try to make our lives better. At the same time, how would you spend your time if you knew that there was a limit to how much wellbeing money could give you? In an extreme sense, some of the happiest, strongest people I've met in the world actually have nothing. I'm not talking about *Singapore nothing*, I'm talking about *village in the middle of East Timor nothing*, which is really nothing. I guess I've been very inspired by the people I've met who taught me about the simplicity of living. They showed me how, especially in Singapore, we can be blinded by what we think we need.

I was recently reading an article about the !Kung Bushmen, which is a tribe in Africa.[30] When anthropologists studied this tribe in the 1970s, they noticed that they didn't have access to

---

[30] Stasja Koot and Bram Büscher, "Giving Land (Back)? The Meaning of Land in the Indigenous Politics of the South Kalahari Bushmen Land Claim, South Africa','

groundwater or possessions. From the perspective of the anthropologists back then, they concluded that these people are in abject poverty. They lead lives of desperation because they don't have these things. 40 years later, the field of anthropology was more advanced, and another team of anthropologists went back to study the !Kung Bushmen again. Now instead of looking at their lives from the perspective of the anthropologist, they tried to see things from the perspective of the !Kung Bushmen. They found that the !Kung Bushmen did not believe in the concept of personal property. What the village owns, everyone owns together. Which kind of is a crazy idea because we live in a society where we do not share what we have. It's sort of like asking the fish to get out of the water to look at the fishbowl itself; to start questioning the premise of the fishbowl. I guess I've been lucky that the people I've met and the work I'm involved in has constantly allowed me to do that. Sorry for the very long-winded answer, it's a tough question.

[Navin laughs]

DO YOU FEEL RICH?

Si Qi

I want to pick your brain a little bit. I recently interviewed this lady who shared with me how, through her line of work, she observed that many people were living beyond their means with little savings at the end of every month. They lived in condos, hired a maid, drove nice cars. But when they were met with a crisis, they were very badly affected. In this case, it was retrenchment and unemployment.

in *Journal of Southern African Studies* 42, no. 2 (2019): 357–374, doi:10.1080/0305707
0.2019.1605119

I think if you put us in a village where we don't see skyscrapers, we don't see millionaires, we don't understand the concept of money, we wouldn't even think of chasing after these things. But in this environment, many of us feel the need to do so. In that interview, I asked her if there was a better way for us to live. From your work, what do you think we can do to avoid landing in such a situation?

Navin

So there's a really well-known study on relational wealth[31] that took two groups of students from Ivy League University in the US, and gave them two scenarios to choose from. In the first scenario, you earn \$100,000 but everyone around you earns \$80,000. In the second scenario, you earn \$200,000 but everyone around you earns \$280,000. Which one would you pick? Which do you think was the more popular choice?

Si Qi

Ah . . . This is like reverse psychology now!

Navin

It's not! So this was an actual study that was done.

[short pause]

Si Qi

Ahh, tough question, tough question.

MK

Is it the latter?

---

[31] Romesh Diwan, "Relational Wealth and the Quality of Life'," *The Journal of Socio-Economics* 29, no. 4 (2000): 305–40. doi:10.1016/s1053-5357(00)00073-1

Si Qi

I would choose the second scenario.

Navin

Yeah so, that's the thing, right? Logically you would say that earning $200 is better than $100, right? I mean it's logical. But most of the people in this study picked the first scenario.

What this study was trying to demonstrate is that when we think of the concept of wealth, we don't realize that wealth is relational. It is proportional to what is around us.

In Singapore, most of us live in HDB[32] flats. Let's say that you live in a condo and you are in the top 20 per cent of Singapore's economic class. The question is, do you feel rich? And that is a harder question to answer because it depends on what you're comparing yourself to. I can feel rich because I'm talking to you guys now on a MacBook Pro. But I could also think that I'm quite poor because I've been using the same laptop for ten years.

Contentment in Singapore is sometimes misunderstood as, *oh, you basically want to not work for anything lah, you're just happy living your life free and easy*. But that isn't contentment. Contentment means that we go through life looking at motivation not from an extrinsic point of view but from an intrinsic point of view.

Going back to the condo example, if you bought a condo because *all my siblings bought nice houses, I don't want to be left behind*, then in a way you're still living in poverty because you are pinning your idea of what it means to be wealthy on others. But if you said that, *Hey, my children really, really love swimming. Since we can't get access to a pool very often in a HDB flat, maybe if I move to a condo, my children can blossom as swimmers*. In both instances you're buying a condo, but the motivation is very different.

---

[32] HDB: Housing Development Board (Public housing in Singapore)

What I'm just trying to say is that it's not so much about the condo itself. It's what your life is fuelled by and what your actions are underpinned by. If you can unpack that then you start to see if you're actually wealthy or poor, because it's a state of mind.

One study looked at how people's incomes compared with those of people who were similar, and found that 'individuals are happier the larger their income is in comparison with the income of the reference group'[33]. It found that 'the income of the reference group is about as important as one's own income for individual happiness'.

FINDING THAT INTRINSIC MEANING WITHIN US

Si Qi

How do you think we can find that intrinsic meaning or value within us?

Navin

We live in a very exciting time. This call is happening between us, and there is a growing body of work that is becoming more popular now compared to twenty years ago.

Like anything else, one has to first discover the motivation of why. *Why is this important to you?* We can start by looking at people who are very motivated. Let's say we look at the top performers in their field, earning good salaries and all that. Conceivably they're very motivated right? But what is their true motivation?

For me, I think true motivation is the grandma who feeds the stray cats at the HDB blocks every day. And she might not have a lot in life, yet she feels compelled to take care of the cats. There are many people who quietly go about doing the work they do without any recognition.

---

[33] Ada Ferrer-i-Carbonell, "Income and Well-being: an Empirical Analysis of the Comparison Income Effect', *Journal of Public Economics* 89, no. 5-6 (2002), 997–1019, doi:10.1016/j.jpubeco.2004.06.003

These are people who have very strong motivations. I think what unites them is that they've all decided to give themselves to an idea that extends beyond their lifetime. There's a Greek proverb that says that *a society grows great when old men plant trees whose shade they know they shall never sit in.* I often see people picking up litter they didn't throw. It's quite heartening to see people trying to give back in their own small ways to a cause larger than their own lives. Your *why* doesn't have to be something very grand. If we can develop the curiosity to explore the meaning of life beyond what society tells us, that's a great start.

There's a great Greek idea on happiness I personally love. The Greeks have an interesting distinction of happiness. There are two words they use: hedonic happiness and eudaimonic happiness. For hedonic happiness—let's say we like pizza. When we're really hungry, the first slice of pizza we have feels good. When we eat the whole pizza, we feel full. If we finish a second pizza, we'll feel really sick. Now if you ate a third pizza, you'll probably vomit. That's hedonic happiness, it's defined as happiness that depletes as you consume it.

The other word, eudaimonic, is about happiness that only grows as you consume it. For example, if the person at the HDB block feeds one kitten, she's happy. Let's say this person decides to go to SPCA[34] and feed all 20 animals, they're happy. And let's say this person managed to convince the government to give them a grant to support all the animals in Singapore, they'll feel even more happy.

So both of these cases depict pursuits of happiness, but the difference is in one case you cannot consume beyond a certain point, and in fact it makes you sick. In the other case you can actually pursue that happiness to an unlimited degree. That's the

---

[34] SPCA: Society for the Prevention of Cruelty to Animals

difference. By making this distinction, you can start to choose things that really improving your wellbeing in the long run.

HAPPINESS IS A RESULT OF PRACTICE

MK

How do you think Singaporeans can start developing an understanding about resilience, about values, about happiness, in a way that looks inwards rather than looking outwards?

Navin

We don't talk about having happiness or getting happiness. Happiness is the by-product of practices. Sometimes when I hear parents tell kids, *I just want you to be happy*, I do think that it's actually a very corrosive thing. Have you guys seen the movie *Inside Out*?

MK & Si Qi

Yes.

Navin

So the premise of that movie was that Joy, the character, was trying to push Sadness away. What they realized towards the end of the film was that Sadness played such an important role in allowing the child to make sense of her life events. Through Sadness, the child was able to find happiness and meaning.

In The Contentment Foundation, what we do is that we don't talk about happiness, we talk about wellbeing because people who are sad can actually also be well. When I was three or four years old in kindergarten, I was underneath a tree crying. A teacher came up to me and said, 'Hey, boys don't cry, go back to class'. It was just that one line. Through my teenage years and in my twenties, I found it very hard to cry. I can cry now because I learned why it's important to express emotions, but for many people who can't cry, they can never connect with what they're feeling inside. When you numb one feeling, you numb all feelings. It's also why in the foundation, we don't talk about positive and negative emotions. We talk about pleasant and unpleasant emotions because all emotions tell us something. One of the ideas that we could share in Singapore is that happiness is not a destination, it's the by-product of cultivating a healthy mind and heart and cultivating a way of seeing.

And I think that is hard because many people are very averse to pain and discomfort. I think that's something everybody chases after, that so-called 'happiness'. If we truly understand that happiness is a by-product, it really shifts how we view the world and the things we do.

Going back to your point on connecting to difficult emotions, one of the beauties of pain or aching is that it's a sign of growth. If you go to a gym and you do a good workout the next day your muscles might ache. The ache is not comfortable, but it's also a sign of growth. So the problem with too much comfort as well is that we can never truly explore what it means for us to grow in a psychological, spiritual or emotional sense as well.

Si Qi

Yeah, absolutely. So I think this is really tied to resilience because if people are not able to go through difficult periods, they would try to numb it with things like shopping or socializing because the reality is too painful. But in my own journey as well, I've learned that it takes a lot of resilience and patience to sit with yourself through very difficult times. How do you think we can teach children or even adults about resilience?

Navin

I want to go back to the motivation piece because people who don't understand why it's important to explore this will never really be able to explore the idea of resilience.

When you think about the American invasion of Vietnam, the Viet Cong were fighting this vastly superior army which had more advanced technology. But in the end, the Americans left Vietnam not having achieved the objective of why they went to war. So how did an army that was vastly outnumbered and technologically inferior, stay so resilient throughout the war? And the simple thing is that what they were fighting for was clearer to them than it was for the Americans.

In a similar sense, *what are you fighting for?* I think another important piece about this is whether you are serving an idea that is larger than your life. Because it moves away from the egocentric view of *what's in it for me* to *what am I trying to do that lasts beyond my own lifespan?* That, to me, is the foundation to build resilience.

Being able to create groups of people that also resonate with these ideas and to share and practice these concepts together, things like meditation, group therapy, couples counselling, or coaching, all of these things are helpful if you have friends and a support system around you who are also interested in looking at their own lives in a more critical way. So find people that resonate with these ideas and support them on their journey as they support you on yours and explore together as a group.

CHAPTER 12

Gym Training for the Mind

By Sufian Yusof, General Manager, Aileron Wellness

Through working with athletes as a sports coach, Sufian started to realize that it is not just the physical body that affects an athletes' performance, but their mental and emotional state as well. As a result, his work with athletes now goes beyond just managing their physical condition, but to also offer help in their lives outside of the training room. Sufian shares that there is a clear distinction between mental illness and mental wellness, the former which refers to diagnosable conditions, and the latter which refers to our everyday mental states. Just as we would visit a nutritionist if we want to improve our physical wellness, visiting a therapist or receiving medical treatment for our mental health should not carry any stigma in society.

MANAGING EXTERNAL AND INTERNAL STRESSORS

MK

Why not share a little bit about what you're doing right now?

Sufian

I'm a coach in sports performance, and at the same time I'm a lecturer in sports science as well. Training people, developing athletes, and managing them has been a huge part of my life for the last ten years. And down the line, how I view these athletes has changed. I'm not just looking at how they can improve physically from a training programme, but also how they evolve as a person because being in this industry, I get to know them as people. And it's never a short-term relationship with the athletes or students that I work with. The training can span over many years, so I can see the evolution of who they are and the identity they forge for themselves. From there, I get to see the wholeness of the person beyond who they are recognized for in the particular sport.

Si Qi

Especially from a physical health, sports performance perspective, what got you interested in the mental health side of people?

Sufian

That's a really good question. When we talk about training, for example, or we look at the physical aspects of a person, we tend to neglect who they are on the mental aspects. Especially in very high-demand situations, we talk about how they respond to challenges and stress. And when we talk about stress, there are so many different kinds of stress as well. There's internal stress, there's external stress. And the thing is, we manage external stress well, which refers to the physical rigour of training. That's something we can control, but internal stress is something that we don't really acknowledge because we don't really understand much about it. But internal stress is as important to every single individual, not just athletes. Your internal stress has to have a homeostasis and a good balance with your external stress as well, because your internal stress affects your physical body's recovery system.

That's what I've found with my athletes. I use data to track their recovery and sometimes the data picks up on the stress that they've been going through. If they're in a particularly stressful situation, be it internal or external, for example, their resting heart rate might go up a little bit. So those kinds of qualitative and quantitative data tells me that *okay, I need to manage different aspects of their lives properly*. Because from a physical standpoint, if your resting heart rate is up, it tells me that you can't perform well, and that's going to affect your training. Down the line, it can compound into something even bigger if you don't manage it well. So I think that's where I started to see the bigger picture of not just managing their external stress but also looking at their internal stresses, the things they do in life, their identity, and their relationship with everything around them. I think that's really important because anecdotally, I find that if I manage their internal stress well, they can actually deal with external stress better. So the whole mindfulness aspect and looking at where they are in terms of their mental space really is the bigger picture for me, rather than just their physical performance.

MK

I am very stressed out now . . .

[laughter]

Sufian

As we all are. (laughing) So how you respond to it also is important right?

MK

Exactly. Let's talk a bit about COVID. Because when the lockdown happened, our work and personal spaces collapsed and we no longer had our usual breathing spaces. It all became one space. In the past, at least we had some breathing space between home and work. There was some time in between. Even if it's forty-five minutes, it's still a breathing space for us to adjust and adapt. But when COVID happened, all the spaces collapsed and it became very confusing for some because all of our roles started getting tangled up together.

Sufian

I totally understand that. I think that's where the lines between who you are and the different roles you have to fulfil become blurry. And I think from the context of COVID, for example, the different roles that you have to fulfil become a very grey area. For me, how do I function as a husband? How do I function as an employee or a teacher at home?

MK

So we're talking about roles. How we distinguish the roles and the functions we play on a day-to-day basis can allow us to have the segregation, the mental categorization, and the emotional space to pack things in their respective boxes.

Sufian

Correct. I think compartmentalization is tricky as well because sometimes, with the different roles you have to play, it becomes difficult to stay rooted to who you are and I think not many people can do it well, or they tend to struggle with it. Sometimes, it's not within themselves to hold their own. They sort of conform to what society thinks—

MK

The expectations that are being imposed on them, whether it is from society, family, organization, family, partners, or even themselves. And something we are not really conscious about is the kind of expectations being placed onto us. We live in a very fast pace of life and we don't really have the space to breathe and re-examine the question of *who am I? What matters to me at my core?*

Sufian

I think that's really important, talking about the core of who you are. I'm a huge believer in the environment shaping who you are as a person. Beyond genetics—because genetics might have a role to play—more often than not, it's the environment that shapes who you are right to the core of your being, your centre. So I think that's why a lot of people are going through a tough time during COVID because they don't have the essence of *what's my core? How do I fulfil all these roles to the best of my ability? At the same time, how can I make sure that in society's eyes, people can still see that I'm fulfilling these roles well enough?* So I think that's the challenging part that we've faced in the last one-and-a-half years. It actually makes or breaks us.

MK

Got it. Now, can you tell us a little bit more about the work that you do with the athletes in the organization?

Sufian

So for me, apart from just the training aspect, I look at their personal life as well, so I tend to form very close relationships with my athletes. External stress is something that I can easily control and measure, but the internal stress is what really makes or breaks an athlete. That's why for me, I will try to have a good relationship with them, but for that to happen, they have to trust me first. They have to let me into their lives, and from there, what I'll do is help them manage their internal stresses based on who they are in terms of their personality, in terms of their emotions, and their identity as well.

We talked about different roles, right? The same goes for athletes too. Most athletes have different roles to play and in Singapore's context, not all athletes are training full-time. They have a job, they have their own families, some of them are still in school. And the thing is all these roles they play contribute to their internal stress. In that sense, I help them manage their stresses individually according to the roles that they have to play. So, if they're an athlete, what can they control? Again, it's all about trying to control what they can control. What can they do to ensure they're in the right headspace? If they're a student feeling stressed out about exams? What can they control to manage their stress when it comes to exams? If they're a son who needs to take care of his parents, what are the things he can control to fulfil his role as a son? My relationship with them goes beyond just the sports or the training room. It's to really make sure that they identify who they are as person beyond their role as an athlete, and to see that *outside of this training, I am this person, I have to play all these roles, I have to manage them well enough so that they don't affect me or compound into something that's worse.*

I've always believed that when it comes to mental health, it's never a one-off thing, right? It's never one trigger. It's a combination of so many triggers that eventually you'll reach a boiling point, then you'll act upon it. So before we even get to that stage, we have to make sure that we are managing all these little things well enough so that we don't ever think about going there.

THE FIRST STEP IS ACKNOWLEDGEMENT

MK

And what are some of the mental stigmas you have observed?

Sufian

Generally, we don't really address mental health as it is. In the past, we tend to brush it off. And if you ask me, there is a clear distinction between mental illness and mental wellness but I think we still don't understand the distinctions well enough. We tend to categorize them into one basket.

MK

How would you define them?

Sufian

For me, when we look at mental illness and mental wellness, it depends on the context. For example, if you look at the context of mental illness, we can talk about genetics or a chemical imbalance or deficiency. It's the same as food. Some people have iron deficiency, so they take iron pills. Or they have a certain vitamin deficiency, so they take vitamin B supplements. But when it comes to mental illness, if you have a serotonin deficiency and you are required to take medication, people will then brand you as someone who's 'crazy'. Sometimes we are quick to judge when it comes to mental illness even though we don't really understand where it's coming from and the context behind it. Much like physical illnesses, there are underlying factors that can be identified through clinical diagnosis for mental illnesses, which can then be addressed through the appropriate treatment methods, be it medication, therapy, or a combination of both.

When it comes to mental wellness, we go through different emotions every day and it's fine to have those different emotions. I think where society fails is that we are afraid to acknowledge those emotions. We are afraid to acknowledge that we are feeling burnt out because of the potential judgement we might receive from our bosses who may think that we are being lazy or slacking off. So mental wellness, to me, is about managing your day-to-day emotions and how you acknowledge them. The first step to understanding or improving your mental wellness is actually to acknowledge it, knowing that it is fine. As a society, we have yet to reach that stage where it's okay to acknowledge the kinds of emotions we go through. That's because, like I said, we tend to put everything in one basket. Everything is 'crazy' when it comes to mental health regardless of how serious it is.

Si Qi

I think it's interesting because when it comes to emotions, you talk about acknowledging it being the first step, but more often than not we tend to either brush it aside or suppress it. And we think that it goes away, or we think that just because *I don't think about it anymore that means that it's not really affecting me.* But then the emotions are bubbling somewhere and it's affecting us in some way shape or form, and it actually makes things worse if you don't acknowledge it.

Sufian

It's also the stigma that deters people from speaking to professionals, especially in an Asian context. And the thing is, if the first step is to acknowledge it, then the next step is to know the right people to talk to. Let's go back to my previous example of nutrition deficiency. If you have nutrition deficiency, you talk to a nutritionist and the nutritionist will come out with a guideline for you to manage it and to see how you can cope with the deficiency through various lifestyle interventions. The same should apply to mental wellness—seeking help and talking to a professional should be as easy and accessible and judgement-free as talking to a nutritionist and coming up with lifestyle interventions to manage it well. I think that's where a lot of people are afraid as they don't want to be seen as someone who is in serious need of help. Whereas if you ask me, talking to a counsellor is just talking to a professional to manage my emotions well, that's it.

And it ends there; it doesn't define who I am as a person. It's just getting professional advice and talking about the things I'm not so sure about.

If you ask any layman on the street from a general knowledge standpoint, how well do they really know the different emotions? What's anxiety to them? What's stress to them? What's burnout to them?

MK

It's the same thing as what I told you in our previous conversations. We've been trained in school to use our head, but no one ever taught us how to use our heart. We don't really understand our emotions. We think that we're feeling happy, we think that we're feeling sad, we think that we're feeling angry. But what we don't recognize is that emotions also have layers as well. And we can experience a multitude of emotions all at once—that you can feel angry, happy, and sad all at the same time. But because we were not trained, we don't understand our internal psyche, there's no way for us to compartmentalize. There's no emotional vocabulary to even distinguish and define them.

Sufian

I think that's a systemic issue as well. You mentioned schools and being taught from young—we're taught to behave a certain way or to pick up certain negative connotations with different emotions. Being angry is bad, being sad is not good, you always have to see the positive things in life, you always have to be happy all the time. That becomes a problem as we get older because now you don't know how to address it. Nobody taught us how to manage our anger or sadness.

MK

Yeah. Without sadness, how can we truly know what happiness is? We don't recognize that these emotions are part of the scale, and we get so fixated about wanting to be happy all the time. No wonder we're not satisfied.

Sufian

Yeah, that is true. I mean again, I think it's a bit of a systemic fault—who we are as a society, our culture. I think all of this plays a huge role in defining the kind of people that we eventually become when we go out into society. All this has to be addressed from a very young age and we have to have a system that allow us to talk openly about our emotions. We need to address that it is okay to go through a spectrum of emotions.

I also think that it's really important to have a generation of people who are empathetic. That's important because understanding emotions brings us one step closer to being empathetic, and eventually, it helps you get closer to finding your core. If you always hide behind a mask and you don't acknowledge certain behaviours or certain feelings, then when the going gets tough, it gets really hard to address the situation. That's why, as a society, we have to start acknowledging this from a very young age.

CREATING CHANGE FROM A TOP-DOWN APPROACH

MK

What are some things you think we can do, whether it is on an individual level, or whether it is on a community level, to reduce these stigmas and raise awareness about mental health, their emotional wellness, and also their physical health as well?

Sufian

Good question, but a very hard one as well, because it has to come from both a top-down and bottom-up approach if you ask me. I think in Singapore's context, we are very much driven by a top-down approach, so anything that has to improve has to come from that. I might be wrong, but this is what I feel, because whatever directives that we get, whatever narratives that we get, it is always from a top-down approach, whether it is from the government or an authority figure. So they have to come out with something first, if you ask me. They have to be the ones to drive mental health initiatives so that it becomes a norm.

In Singapore, we very much have a herd mentality. And I think, fair play to us, because this herd mentality has served us well and we are doing a decently good job at managing COVID collectively, right? I think from the mental health standpoint, it's a similar approach. We are now having conversations that were difficult to talk about just five or six years ago, which is a good step. It's a very small step, but it's the first step to becoming better as a society.

Now the next question is about what's next, right? Now that we're talking about this, how do we progress on to the next phase? And it's still more of, from a top-down approach, what can our leaders do to drive the next phase of things? So raising awareness is one thing, but now that you have this awareness, how do you want to manage these issues? What are the initiatives or the help you can get to reduce judgement or reduce the impact it has on you as a person, or on your livelihood? There was a big conversation about removing the need to declare mental health conditions on hiring forms—

MK

Work application.

Sufian

Yeah, and it was removed in 2020. I think it's about those kinds of things that are driven from a top-down approach.

Going back to the idea of herd mentality, it's also about having a sense of belonging and a tribe, knowing that I'm not the only one with an issue. If I'm depressed, I'm not the only one in this situation. I think it's really important that you know that people are there for you. A lot of people feel lonely when it comes to their own mental health. But we are all humans. We are social creatures, no matter what. You might say that you're introverted or extroverted but at the end of the day, we are still social creatures, and we want to be accepted. If we are defined by or labelled by who we are depending on our mental state, then we're not going to go far. So we need to make sure that we have an accepting society that accepts everyone beyond just a label.

MK

Any last words you want to leave to the people, to whoever's reading this to ponder about?

Sufian

For whoever's reading this, and to whoever's going through a very tough period in your life, it's okay to feel that way. It's okay to have difficult emotions, and it's okay to acknowledge them. Just know that there are people out there who can be your source of support. Sometimes we talk about finding your friends or finding your loved ones to talk to, but they may not be the best people to give you advice regarding the challenges you face. So know that you're not alone. Know that there's someone out there to help you if you need it. Speak to a professional. There's nothing wrong with that, and the first step is to acknowledge that this is okay. And the next step is learning, with the help of a professional, how to manage it. And eventually, I hope this gets you to a better place.

CHAPTER 13

Paying More Attention: The Role of the Body in Mental Health

By Daphne Chua, Registered Yoga and Somatic Therapist, Movement Educator and Therapeutics Trainer, Somatic Therapy Asia

Daphne often works with clients to help them release pain and tension in their bodies. Her work involves looking at a person as whole, and not just their physical conditions or presenting symptoms. The body is a gateway to understanding our relationship with ourselves, our lifestyle, or what we hope to change. Having the space to restore, destress, and notice what is around us and our relationship to the world, is a key element in developing better mental and emotional states.

USING THE PHYSICAL BODY AS A GATEWAY

Daphne

After being overseas for over a decade, I returned home after the sudden passing of my father, mainly to be close to family again, now that I've only got one parent left. I think that coming back to Singapore also meant that I could actually try to kind of hack the traditional healthcare system. I'm not really an activist and I'm not here to revolutionize the medical system. I think that perhaps one day we can find enough people to collaborate with and drive that change, but I'm not that kind of champion. I simply enjoy the interactions with people who come and see me to fix their back pain, and at the same time, start to uncover so much about themselves and see that they're not just their back pain.

MK

Tell me more about that.

Daphne

I combine yoga therapy with bodywork and somatic. So we really look at the person as a whole entity, not just their physical conditions or presenting symptoms. We use the body as a gateway to create curiosity—What is your relationship with your body? What's your lifestyle? What are you hoping to change? We're human beings—we're never content. Whenever somebody tells me that 'My life is great, that I'm super content' . . . It's not that I don't believe them. I do, but I also know that it takes a lot of inner work to really mean what you say.

We use the physical body as a gateway to the mental, emotional, and spiritual being. Spiritual, but not in a religious sense. I'm not religious. I don't believe that there's a man sitting in the sky putting us together part by part. I believe we're grown from a seed, and the forces of nature and nurture make us who we are right now. It's just like tending to a plant. You look at the soil, at how much sunlight it's getting. You look at the environment, at the surrounding vegetation. So why can't we also treat human beings or even any form of sentient being in that way? To look at the order of things, at the bigger, greater energy that binds us. Let's start with gravity. What's our relationship with gravity? Really pay attention and hone your awareness to your relationship with the people and things around you. When we examine our relationships, we can get more insights on how we can trust ourselves, trust the order of things, and trust gravity. We don't have to fight or struggle with everything that comes our way.

A lot of joint pains and autoimmune diseases come with our innate sense of fight and flight. We fight with gravity and try to run away from it because we don't trust it. When that happens, we go into a state of un-centred-ness and un-grounded-ness. This physiological state of ungroundedness will show itself up in the body through our weak links like our lower back, our neck and shoulders, our knees, and et cetera.

MK

What do you think is the importance of the role the body plays in relation to mental health?

Daphne

One of my favourite teachers is Bonnie Bainbridge Cohen. She's the founder of Body Mind Centering®, on which I have based a lot of my work. If I can quote her, maybe not verbatim, but she says that the mind is like the wind, and the body is like the sand. When you want to know where the wind is blowing, look at the sand. Therefore, the body is the imprint of our mental and emotional state.

If we are in fight or flight mode, or if we have had trauma, our body is going to be in a state of untethered-ness. This is when we become tunnel-visioned and narrow-minded—when we think the whole world revolves around our suffering and pain, whether it's stress from work, from home, or loneliness, or trauma. Whenever someone is stressed out, anxious, depressed, or disassociated, they feel very alone—as if no one else will truly understand them, as if no one else suffers like them. And this aloneness can manifest in the body as a fear of change, distrust, or self-sabotage, for example. But if we don't trust, how are we going to trust allowing our body to relax? We subconsciously think that *I can't relax because that means I have to let my guard down.*

So we brace, our body tightens up, and our breath becomes shallow and short. When that happens, our organs also start to feel that stress. It's not getting enough time to rest, or our nervous system doesn't get the space to restore, to destress, to digest. And the cycle perpetuates.

In somatic therapy or in bodywork, we look at things like how well your organs are working and maybe even how bloated you are feeling. Maybe your back pain is caused by your organs sitting in the front of the body because your body is not providing a conducive environment for them to function and move properly. This happens when your nervous system can't get into the parasympathetic state that allows it to go into rest and digest mode. So your organs become inanimated and frozen. And they're sitting at the front of your abdominal cavity, pulling into your lower back.

So oftentimes, I ask people, when was the last time you pooped? How was your sleep? I know nowadays there's a lot of technology that can track how well you sleep, but a device only shows you statistics. How are you deciphering it? What kind of stories can it tell you? If there are some patterns you're noticing, what are they telling you about your state of being? If you know that you tend to have certain patterns or habits, perhaps it would be more apparent if you don't trust gravity, that you are not able to let go, which causes your body and mind to resist sleep.

MK

We are always holding certain tensions in our body.

Daphne

Now, say, if you're in a session with me, and I lift your legs and ask if you can trust and allow yourself to receive the touch and support so that you don't have to hold your legs up with your own effort, can you trust me to hold your legs for you?

MK

And that's how the practice of relaxation came about. Are you able to let go?

There's a saying the heart knows what the mind knows not, but I'm going to add something. The body knows what the heart knows not. The body knows what the mind knows not.

Daphne

I also feel that coming back to Singapore now, and throughout the years as I came back for visits, I realize that there is a changing landscape. COVID definitely brought mental health into the limelight, which is a good thing, because there has been so much stigma, and there still is, but much less. People always think someone is siao. Seeing a therapist was such a taboo.

Take the arts scene in Singapore for example. Being an artist, perhaps during the 1990s and early 2000s, was always something that you could afford to do only if you were from a particular social stratum because you didn't need to conform to the aspiration of 'earning big bucks'. Right now, the gap is closing. There is definitely still that accessibility issue, but at the same time, it is now more acceptable. It is no longer *you're a good-for-nothing*. It is no longer *because you cannot be a doctor, a lawyer, or an engineer, then you become an artist*. That was how things were during my time.

Now, it's different. Our whole mindset is different, and the world is changing. It's okay to be different, to be in the left field. And that's a good thing.

CHALK AND CHEESE

MK

I like how, when you said that, the sun suddenly showed up and now, it's super bright.

Daphne

It's a great thing. But at the same time, everything that is good is always—

MK

It's a double-edged sword.

Daphne

Yes, and I think the flip side of that is that there are a lot more people who call themselves healers and artists but don't really embody that. Or they don't really understand what it means. And because it's more and more young people—and I say this with not a tinge of malice—whose minds are brilliant, along with information being very accessible, it's very easy to acquire the intellectual knowledge of these deep concepts. But to embody it comes with a lot more experience and humility, and I find that that is lacking, especially in Singapore, amongst the practitioners here.

You can go and study papers or whatever, but it's not regulated. So you can be whatever, do whatever, call yourself whatever. Because it's not regulated, you get a lot of people doing this kind of stuff now, and wellness has turned into a thriving and lucrative industry.

I think right now, there's the question of quality versus quantity. The problem is people are not educated enough to discern that. And secondly, there's a lot of education that we need to cultivate or create in terms of educating the general population on how to look at their condition, their illness, or their disease. There's another gap there which is right now, healthcare professionals and therapists or wellness practitioners are like chalk and cheese. They don't talk to each other, they criticize each other's practice a lot, and they're always at odds.

MK

They're very divided.

Daphne

It's very, very divided. In an ideal world, they should complement each other.

MK

That's what I built ThisConnect for. It was also to connect and bring mental health professionals together because the resources allocated to the cause are limited, and we are especially more divided. I don't think it's a wrong statement to make; many mental health professionals are just doing their own thing in their own capacity. They may have the heart for the work, but due to the imbalanced demand and supply, and coupled with the lack of resources being pumped into the industry, more often than not, they face the risk of burning out. And there isn't strong enough synergy for these professionals to even come together to double or triple up and amplify their intentions towards the cause. I think more must be done if we want to see real transformation happening on the ground, from the individual to collective level, where mental health is concerned.

I want to add on to what you just said, especially when it comes to learning about emotions. We've been trained in school on how to use our brains, but no one ever taught us how to use our hearts. Our ability to feel is so limited. So, oftentimes, when it comes to dealing with difficult emotions, we get stuck. We don't think that anger, sadness, and happiness can all come together at the same time. We don't even recognize that there are layers inside those emotions.

REFRAMING VULNERABILITY AS STRENGTH

Daphne

Asian societies are generally very repressed. We're told to not show our feelings because it's a sign of weakness, that vulnerability is weakness. But I think the bigger conversation should be about reframing vulnerability as strength. The ability to be vulnerable is actually very courageous. If you can be honest with yourself and you can find the sensory vocabulary to emote—and it doesn't have to be verbal, which is where things like art, music and movement therapy can come in because they offer different channels to emote and express—it gives you choices, and choices give you freedom.

Freedom is not the ability to do whatever you want at any given point in time. Freedom is having the curiosity to trust, the courage to be vulnerable, and the wisdom to know that there is something that's much greater as a community. Then it becomes faith, and we can lean into the support of forces that are greater than us—like gravity. The order of nature is the reason why we're born. It's the reason why the sun comes up. It's the reason why birds sing. But most people don't pay attention to that anymore, and we really should.

CHAPTER 14

Coming to Therapy is Only Half the Work

By Rachel Yang, Registered Art Psychotherapist, Co-Founder of Daylight Creative Therapies, President of Singapore Association of Art Therapy

The first thing about therapy is making a conscious choice to be there. Therapy can be intense as it encourages you to look at yourself and examine patterns and behaviours that may no longer be serving you. Going to therapy is only part of the work, the rest of the work is done outside of the therapeutic space through reflection and processing. Rachel believes in making small shifts that can slowly be cultivated into healthier patterns and ways of being. She highlights that self-awareness as a reflective practice encourages us to examine ourselves, and cultivate practices that contribute positively to our mental and emotional wellbeing.

MAKING SMALL SHIFTS THROUGH ART THERAPY

MK

You were previously working as a graphic designer. What made you switch over to art therapy?

Rachel

I was working as a graphic designer for fifteen years and found that I wasn't fulfilled by my job. I was interested in doing psychology. However, I was unable to find anything that resonated with me. I researched different psychology degrees for about three years until I came across the Masters in Art Therapy course at LASALLE College of the Arts, and that completely changed my life. I signed up for a talk at the college which was open to the public, and after two hours, I came out, and I knew that this was absolutely the only thing I wanted to be doing. I enrolled, was accepted, and have not looked back since. That was seven years ago.

MK

What kind of issues do people come to you for when they join an art therapy session?

Rachel

In Daylight Creative Therapies, we get a number of issues. Predominantly adults with anxiety, depression, self-harm and suicidal ideation, eating disorders, and anger management. We also see children with emotional dysregulation and stress from school.

MK

So what exactly is art therapy, and how does this modality allow people to resolve the issues they're facing?

Rachel

So art therapy, or art psychotherapy, is the combination of psychotherapy with art. We use art as a tool. We focus on the process and the biopsychosocial aspects of a client's life. We're not just looking at one thing; we're looking at family history, engagement with peers, how they may be functioning in their day-to-day lives.

We believe in making small shifts rather than big changes because when you make big changes, they are oftentimes hard to keep up with and people tend to slip back and feel worse about themselves because they've tried to make this big change and it hasn't worked. We believe in making small shifts each day, and it can be as simple as getting up and having a shower.

MK

So it comes from habitual disciplines?

Rachel

It comes from being gentle with yourself and allowing yourself to get through each day without feeling worthless, without feeling like you're not contributing to the world. That can start from something small. It can come down to even watering a plant—it's a very simple process.

In our practice, we encourage clients to keep a visual journal as part of their process. A visual journal is a repository of thoughts, feelings, experiences, and expressions. Some clients write a lot in their visual journal, others create more art. Clients sometimes recognize through their visual journal that their emotional states change. This is an important revelation as sometimes, we can feel that we remain in one emotional state for days on end. With a visual journal, clients can see that even though they have been sad for one day, there are other days that they were less sad and depressed. The visual journal enables us to objectively view these constantly moving states.

OPEN CONVERSATIONS ARE THE FIRST STEP

MK

You've worked with diverse groups of people from teenagers, to children, to adults, and even people in shelters and with special needs. What are some of the observations that you've made when it comes to the mental health stigmas in society?

Rachel

As a generation, we're learning to talk about mental health more, but it's not enough. More education about mental health should be addressed in schools. We should be encouraging psychoeducation early on so that people learn to talk about their feelings, learn to ask for help, learn to accept their states, and encourage supportive conversations around suicide and self-harm.

We're a very fast paced society, short-lived based on our social media. We fly through social media and are constantly swiping on to the next thing. I think with the younger generation now, a lot of it is based on how they're being seen in the public eye. So if they're not getting likes, they begin to feel a sense of worthlessness or not being liked because they haven't got as many likes as their friends, or their content isn't as interesting. We often come across youth and adults who are unable to define parts of themselves. They're really struggling with their identity and their place in the world around them.

TRAUMA IMPACTS OUR MIND AND BODY

MK

What are the similarities or patterns that you see when you work with children, teenagers, adults, or people from different demographic groups? Are there any similarities or differences between the different archetypes?

Rachel

There are differences because we're looking at developmental stages when working with individuals across the lifespan. As children, trauma can be integrated into self-perception and, similar to trauma in adults, have long-lasting effects on our physiology, and emotional or mental states.

MK

As compared to adults, what do you think are the differences? You said that the way they perceive traumas is different?

Rachel

Trauma impacts both our mind and body. Trauma has the capacity to rewire our brain and can impact us on a deep level, so it's a very wide question. Trauma can be experienced across the lifespan and can also be experienced as vicarious trauma. This can impact individuals working in places like hospitals as well as mental health practitioners who are working with high-intensity cases. It's important that people in the helping professions also get support.

THERE IS NO HEALTH WITHOUT MENTAL HEALTH

MK

That brings us nicely to the next question. A lot of people are afraid to step inside the therapy room, or they're not sure what therapy is about. They might not know what mental health is. As a mental health professional, could you unpack what mental health is?

Rachel

Mental health is similar to physical health. Without mental health, there's no physical health. If you are unable to get out of bed in the mornings because you don't have motivation in life or feel that your existence is futile, or you live in a chaotic state, you're in survival mode. In this state, you are alive but not engaging and living a well-balanced life. Our mental health should come first.

MK

And what can therapy, or art therapy do for people? There are so many stigmas about stepping into the therapy room because people don't know what to expect, they don't know what therapy is, and they can't be open about it.

Rachel

The first thing about therapy is making a conscious choice to be there. That is 50 per cent of the work. Therapy can be intense as it encourages you to look at yourself and examine patterns and behaviours that may no longer be serving you. Going to therapy is only part of the work, the rest of the work is done outside of the therapeutic space through reflection and processing. We believe in making small shifts that can slowly be cultivated into healthier patterns and ways of being.

Art therapy is psychodynamic in nature and we use art as a tool for creative expression. Through lines, shapes, colours, and different mediums of exploration, we can begin to uncover deeper emotions and understand how they manifest in the present life. No art experience is required in art therapy. Expression can be found in anything from making a mark on a paper, to describing how you're feeling, to tearing up paper, splashing paint, or breaking clay pieces to represent how you may be feeling. It's about expression and learning to look and sit with the pain and discomfort in order to begin to process where that discomfort may have stemmed from so that we may move through it, rather than try to suppress and ignore the feelings. Often times, we are disconnected from the initial pain and mask this pain with unhealthy habits.

THE DISCONNECT STARTS YOUNG

MK

Yes, the lack of connection.

Rachel

The lack of connection within ourselves and from others. So the question is, how do we integrate body and mind? How do we start integrating what is being thought about? Because oftentimes, people with anxiety or depression have ruminating thoughts. This in turn causes stress. It floods the body with cortisol, the stress hormone. Increased levels of cortisol can negatively impact the immune system and increase blood pressure and the risk of heart diseases, to name a few. Understanding that what happens in the mind impacts the rest of our physiology is the first step to learning to become connected to our bodies. We can do this through mindfulness practices, meditation, journaling, exercising, and movement. In therapy, we can begin to explore where discomfort is experienced within the body and what events may trigger somatic experiences.

In art therapy, we use clay, bilateral drawings, and paint on large canvases to begin to explore and express these feelings into physical forms to reflect further on.

MK

Mental health is a very long journey, and we always talk about looking inwards but that's difficult, especially when we've been trained and conditioned to look outwards. When it comes to looking inwards, we don't have a map. We don't know how to even go into ourselves. What do you think are the reasons preventing or holding people back from looking inwards?

Rachel

As mentioned earlier, self-awareness is a reflective practice that encourages us to examine ourselves. And as with all practices, this takes time to cultivate and be open to. Our modern culture is evolving rapidly and unlike in the past where information on others was only available on television, print media and the radio, we now have access to more information than we can handle. We're repeatedly being bombarded by social media where photos or videos depict happy lives and there's a constant need to keep up and be more.

We're busy looking out and while we're hyperconnected, we are disconnected from ourselves and from nature. The destruction of the planet is perhaps the most important part of this conversation because we are not doing enough to save our planet. We need more green spaces, quiet, and calm. We need our planet to exist. The destruction of the planet is reflective of how we are not taking care of ourselves.

MK

We throw rubbish on the ground, just that simple act itself is . . .

Rachel

Yes, and our use of plastic. Like with most things, everything takes time to change.

Research has proven that people feel better after being out in nature and reconnecting with themselves and their surroundings. Perhaps we need to be looking more at how we can be helping the planet and each other rather than trying to live up to superficial expectations. Spend time engaging with one another, reconnecting through family time, and being genuinely interested in what the other party is saying.

Disconnection can start from a young age. With the introduction of mobile devices, children are learning to engage online rather than in person. There are numerous physical and mental health risks that come with the over usage of mobile devices too, such as low IQ and sleep deprivation. Being 'on' all the time further compounds feelings of tiredness and anxiousness.

It's hard to carve out time to spend with kids, especially when parents are working and managing different aspects of life. Different physical activities, engaging with art, and learning tools can support healthy growth in children rather than using their mobile devices.

THERAPY IS A CHOICE

MK

Excellent. My next question is, what is it like behind the scenes of being a therapist? What are the highlights and the lowlights?

Rachel

Ha! That feels like a loaded question! The highlight of being a therapist is engaging with people on a deeply personal level. Being able to be with a person through some of their darkest times. And being present to witness the internal and personal shifts that happen, seeing people have AHA! moments in their sessions, in recognizing behaviours and patterns that may no longer be serving them, and taking steps to move through difficult feelings. Healing takes time. Similar to a journey, it's a process. There is some misconception that coming to a single of session of therapy will provide the answers to problems. This is not how therapy works.

MK

I know! *Can I heal thirty years of emotional baggage in one therapy?*

Rachel

Wouldn't that be amazing! Unfortunately, that's not how it works. As I mentioned, therapy is a process. Shifts and changes take time. It's about working on yourself rather than trying to change situations and people around you.

MK

What are some of the changes you wish to see in the mental health space for both patients and therapists?

Rachel

Firstly, we need more regulations for mental health practitioners so as to safeguard clients. Specifically for art therapists, unlike the US or UK, Singapore does not have a regulatory board. This means that people with some art background may call themselves 'art therapists', which is potentially dangerous and unethical as accredited and credentialed art therapists have gone through rigorous trainings and are required by the credentialing body to be in regular supervision and annual CPD[35] trainings.

For clients, it's important to do background checks and shop around for the right fit with their therapists. There have been cases where the client's trust has been broken from previous experiences with other mental health professionals and they have had to grapple with whether or not to try and approach other therapists.

MK

So the privacy and confidentiality agreements and safe spaces were broken.

Rachel

Yes, but obviously there are more deep-seated issues that have not been addressed. Our first priority is to safeguard our clients.

---

[35] CPD: Continued Professional Development

MK

Got it. How has your personal mental health journey been like as a therapist?

Rachel

As part of our art therapy training, we are required to have regular personal therapy. It's an important part of the training to start addressing underlying issues that we may be unaware of, and also to learn to look at ourselves and reflect. I took a break for a while and recently started seeing a therapist again. It's an important process to examine things that are uncomfortable and be aware of them. We all have ups and downs, and being in therapy helps to tease apart misconceptions, preconceived ideas, and expectations that may be preventing me from living a more connected life. It's an ongoing journey.

Self-care is important. This includes spending time with people close to me and spending time in nature. Part of being human is to reflect, process, and learn to accept parts of ourselves that are less appealing. As human beings, we're intricately flawed. And that is alright. We are constantly learning about ourselves and learning to make more informed choices. Coming into therapy is a choice. Actively participating is a choice. Being patient and kind to ourselves, especially in an ongoing pandemic, is important. Take time out to be still and to reconnect.

The path to finding the answers is not easy by any means, and sometimes the answers aren't what we expect them to be. But there are 1001 reasons not to do something, and you only need one to do it—because **your life matters.** Doors and windows of opportunity open when they do, and it is up to you to step in. If the experience of this book has sparked something deeper in you that you wish to examine, let this be another sign from the universe to keep going.

If you'd like to reach out to have a conversation with us, our doors are open.

Send us a message on Instagram at **@thisconnect.today,** and we'll be happy to connect with you.

Bibliography

Ada Ferrer-i-Carbonell, 'Income and Well-Being: An Empirical Analysis of the Comparison Income Effect.'

Journal of Public Economics 89, no. 5–6 (2005): 997–1019. https://doi.org/10.1016/j.jpubeco.2004.06.003.

Daniel Kahneman and Angus Deaton, 'High Income Improves Evaluation of Life but Not Emotional Well-Being.'

Proceedings of the National Academy of Sciences 107, no. 38 (2010): 16489–93. doi:10.1073/pnas.1011492107.

Daniel Kahneman, Ed Diener, and Norbert Schwarz (Eds.), 'Well-Being: The Foundations of Hedonic Psychology (New York: The Russell Sage Foundation, 1999), Pp. XII + 593.'

Utilitas 18, no. 2 (2006): 192–96. https://doi.org/10.1017/s0953820806231972.

Romesh Diwan, 'Relational Wealth and the Quality of Life.'

The Journal of Socio-Economics 29, no. 4 (2000): 305–40. https://doi.org/10.1016/s1053-5357(00)00073-1.

Stasja Koot and Bram Büscher, 'Giving Land (Back)? the Meaning of Land in the Indigenous Politics of the South Kalahari Bushmen Land Claim, South Africa.'

Journal of Southern African Studies 45, no. 2 (2019): 357–74. https://doi.org/10.1080/03057070.2019.1605119.

Acknowledgements

I would like to express our heartfelt gratitude to all the people who have played a part in making this book come to life. To our contributors, thank you for jumping in and contributing your time, energy, and intention towards forwarding the mental health scene in Singapore. It is a work in progress, and perhaps it may take more than just one lifetime to see the transformation unfold, yet your desire to make a difference to the people out there is instrumental to keeping the vision alive for our future generations, in wellness and prosperity. I am grateful to all of you for the good work that is being done out there and I look forward to more efficient and effective interventions to touch the lives out there.

To the people working with me in the background, Si Qi and Megan, I want to thank you for supporting me in facilitating the process so that these interviews and the backend work could happen. Your beliefs in the cause and my vision, your stand, dedication, and devotion in the project have inspired me to keep going, to push forth to produce a higher quality of work that is nothing less than being impeccable and excellent. This book would not have been completed without your support and commitment.

We embarked on this project with the simple objective to document the different perspectives around mental health in Singapore, yet we walked out of each interview session feeling deeply inspired by selfless acts of service from all these contributors. These interview sessions have shaped our understanding of what service to the community means, no matter big or small, and we deeply cherish the life lessons and personal takeaways we received from all the contributors.

I would also like to attribute and honor all my masters and teachers for being my greatest sources of inspiration for my work, and the trust and faith they placed in me in carrying the work forward to make a difference in this world; trusting in me to do the right thing and getting my act together during my lowest point and being there with me to celebrate my successes and endeavors during my highest peaks. Without them, I would not have been the person I am today. Every single day, I wake up looking forward to live my mark with love, passion and joy.

Finally, I would like to conclude with a quote from Thoreau, Henry David Thoreau, *Walden, or Life in the Woods*:

'I went to the woods because I wished to live deliberately, to front only the essential facts of life, and see if I could not learn what it had to teach, and not, when I came to die, discover that I had not lived. I did not wish to live what was not life, living is so dear; nor did I wish to practice resignation, unless it was quite necessary. I wanted to live deep and suck out all the marrow of life, to live so sturdily and Spartan-like as to put to rout all that was not life, to cut a broad swath and shave close, to drive life into a corner, and reduce it to its lowest terms, and, if it proved to be mean, why then to get the whole and genuine meanness of it, and publish its meanness to the world; or if it were sublime, to know it by experience, and be able to give a true account of it in my next excursion.'

This is an experience we will remember for a lifetime, and we hope that it has inspired you to continue doing the work that you do too. This is only the beginning, and there is so much more to learn, many more steps to take, and much more work to be done.

We hope to honour all our contributors by doing our part to champion mental health causes so that we can create an inclusive, thriving society where people are deeply connected to themselves, to the present, and to the world around them. Thank you.

Acknowledgements

Adrian Pang
Pangdemonium

Amirah Munawwarah
ImPossible
Psychological Services

Andrea Chan
Joel Wong
Lucia Chow
Peggy Lim
TOUCH Community
Services Ltd

Asher Low
Limitless

Belinda Ang
ARTO by thinkART of the
Box Pte Ltd

Brenda Lee
Lynn Tan
The Psychology Practice

Buvenasvari Pragasam
Solace Art
Psychotherapy Pte Ltd

Camellia Wong
InPsychful LLP

Carrie Tan
Nee Soon South
(Nee Soon GRC)

Calvin Eng
Association for
Music Therapy
(Singapore)

Charlotte Goh
Playeum

Cheryl Chan
Fengshan
(East Coast GRC)

Cayden Woo
Jeremy Heng
**Singapore
Children's Society**

Cho Ming Xiu
Campus PSY Limited

Daphne Chua
Somatic Therapy Asia

David Chew
National Heritage Board

David Lim
**Tzu Chi Free Clinic
Special Oral Care Network**

Deborah Seah
Nadera Binte Abdul Aziz
**Community of Peer Support
Specialists (CPSS)**

Desmond Chew
Jacqueline
Jamie
Mysara
Caregivers Alliance Limited

Desmond Soh
Annabelle Psychology

Eric Chua
**Ministry of Culture,
Community and Youth
Ministry of Social and
Family Development**

Etsegenet Mulugeta Eshete
Margaret Hoffer
Selamta Family Project

Goh Li Shan
**REACH (West)
Department of
Psychological Medicine,
National
University Hospital**

Hannah Batrisyia
Muhammad Syazan Bin Saad
Temasek Polytechnic

Jamus Lim
**Anchorvale
(Sengkang GRC)**

Jasmine Yeo
The Private Practice

Jenny Ng
Conscious Parenting Coach
(MEd of Family Education)

Jingzhou
Cassia Resettlement Team

Josephine Chia-Teo
**InSightful Training &
Consultancy Pte Ltd**

John Wong Chee Meng
**Department of
Psychological Medicine,
National
University Hospital**

Jun Lee
**Self-employed
Art Therapist and
Art Facilitator**

Karen Wee
**Lions Befrienders Service
Association**

Kyl Lim
Singapore Cancer Society

Lynette Har
**ICF-Certified Peak
Performance Coach**

Lynette Seow
Safe Space™

Marion Neubronner
**Psychologist
and Leadership
Development Coach**

Michelle Koay
**St. Joseph's Institution
International Ltd**

Murali Pillai
Bukit Batok SMC

Narasimman S/O
Tivasiha Mani
Impart Ltd

Navin Amarasuriya
**The Contentment
Foundation**

Natalie Kang
**Art for Good Pte Ltd
MySpace Psychotherapy
Services Pte Ltd**

Nicole K.
The Tapestry Project SG

Jolene
**Volunteer in the Migrant
Worker Space**

Nur Farhan Bte
Mohammad Alami
Raffles Medical Group

Ng Gim Choo
The EtonHouse Group

Ng Jek Mui
**Dementia Singapore
(formerly known as
Alzheimer's Disease
Association)**

Patrick Tay
Pioneer SMC

Rachel Yang
Daylight Creative Therapies

Ronald P.M.H. Lay
**LASALLE College
of the Arts**

Roshni Bhatia
Yoko Choi
FoundSpace

Seah Kian Peng
**Braddell Heights (Marine
Parade GRC)**

Serene Seng
Senserene Pte Ltd

Siew Kum Yew
Shan You Counselling Centre

Simone Heng
Human Connection Speaker

Sun Kaiying
**Hope for Tomorrow
Psychology Centre**

Sufian Yusof
Aileron Wellness

Tina Hung
**National Council of Social
Service (NCSS)**

Tin Pei Ling
MacPherson SMC

Wan Rizal Bin Wan Zakariah
**Kolam Ayer (Jalan
Besar GRC)**

Vickineswarie Jagadharan
OTHERS

Victor Mills
Michael Chang
Sujata Tiwari
**Singapore International
Chamber of Commerce**

Ying Jie

About THISCONNECT.TODAY

THIS
. CON
NECT

ThisConnect is a mental health advocacy community set up to spark more conscious awareness and forwarding interventions on mental health, emotional wellness, and suicide prevention using experiential art. We recognise the need to begin the mental health conversations by examining the personal struggles that weigh us down in life. These everyday stressors can seem insignificant on their own, but over a long period of time, they can make us feel trapped, lost, stressed, and depressed. Through our work, we want to inspire more people to step out, to connect consciously and deeply with themselves physically, emotionally, mentally and spiritually, and to find the healing with the good and the bad, the positive and the negative, the light and the shadow within them. We want people to access their courage, love, freedom in their beings to express their most authentic selves, and to create a life where they are thriving. We hope that our work will empower individuals to seek help and to look inwards whenever they face challenges in life.

Since 2020, we have presented three large multimedia art exhibitions and thirteen moving satellite shows in Singapore, titled *ThisConnect: Threading Worlds*, Masks of Singapore, and *ThisConnect: What Am I, If I Am Not*, and were featured in *The Straits Times*,

Tatler, Channel 8. Masks of Singapore, a six-month community participatory art project movement, has set the record for the 'Largest Mosaic of Hand-Sculptured Masks' in the Singapore Book of Records and were documented into a photobook with Fujifilm that tells 572 lived-stories of individuals from all walks of lives in their most authentic self behind the masks created.

For more information, reach out at

ThisConnect.today@gmail.com.
https://www.thisconnect.today
https://www.instagram.com/thisconnect.today

'Oftentimes, external expectations about who we should be and how we should act prevent us from being free to express ourselves and do the things that truly matter to us. As a result, many of us end up chasing after societal definitions of success instead of what truly matters to us, and we end up lost, confused, and disconnected from ourselves. It is this disconnection from ourselves that forms the start of the many mental and emotional struggles we face every day, and it is potentially leads to depression, and on a more severe scale, suicide. Through our work, we aim to explore the deeper conversations that underpin the mental health struggles many of us battle in our daily lives and empower people to connect to themselves, to the present, and the world around them. Ultimately, the goal is to see a society where people are free to be bold, be free, and be themselves—unapologetically—so that they can begin to live a life that matters to them.'

Hun Ming Kwang,
Founder, Creative Director,
Author of ThisConnect.today